The New Insider's Guide to Hawaii Volcanoes National Park

After the Eruption!

By
Uldra Johnson

Aloha, e komo mai! Welcome!
Most of the Park has reopened! Yippee!
And it's better than ever!

So you're planning a visit to the land of the most active volcano on planet Earth and the most sacred site in Hawaii!

You will be one of more than 2.5 million people from all over the globe who visits the Big Island each year to witness Earth-in-the-making, an experience that you will never forget!

Molten and congealed lava flows, prehistoric lava tube caves, moon-like steaming calderas, toxic steam clouds lifting hundreds of feet into the blue tropical skies and lava tree molds are set within the pristine, emerald jewel of a rainforest, where rare songbirds and exotic plants that occur no where else on the planet thrive in a virtual Garden of Eden.

Sound exciting?

It is!

Designated an International Biosphere Reserve and a World Heritage Site, the Park, as we locals call it, is also considered by scientists to be the most ideal living laboratory in the world for the study of ecology and geology.

Why?

Because the Hawaiian Islands are the most geographically isolated islands on Earth, and yet this ecological and geographical wonderland is so accessible.

I explore almost daily the many wonders of the Park, on my own as a naturalist and photographer, and as an artist in search of inspiration. I never tire of the incredible beauty of the delicate rainforest and the awesome power of Kilauea Volcano. I love Kilauea, and I truly enjoy sharing this precious natural treasure with others.

3

This guide will take you to my favorite places, tell you where to go, what to look for, and what to take for comfort and safety. You can choose from scenic car stops that overlook steaming calderas or black, frozen lava flows as far as the eye can see, and satisfy your desire for a few moments of eye-candy and photograph-taking, to isolated, rugged camping trails that test your psychological and physical endurance.

Want to sit hidden away beneath the world's tallest ferns in a natural grotto, and listen to the exotic songs of forest birds, and meditate? Or perhaps you feel like exploring among the crystal and rainbow titanium lava shards on the still-steaming floor of a caldera, while rare, majestic Hawaiian hawks soar high above your head?

Maybe you'd like to spend a day wandering and wondering among the more than 20,000 mysterious, ancient petroglyphs carved in an ancient lava flow, each with an enigmatic story to tell?

Then again, you might be the kind to enjoy spelunking through a secreted lava cave with gold and silver icicle-shaped lava stalactites hanging from the roof. It's all here! And much more!

Many visitors to the Park come on the great big buses which virtually whiz through in a few hours, stopping for mere moments at a few convenient places marked "buses only," but if you're reading this guide, you probably are planning a longer, more personalized, more rewarding trip to Kilauea Volcano. Perhaps you are planning to spend more than a day exploring the Park, and I certainly suggest that you do! In that case, you probably will plan to stay in nearby magical Volcano Village, famous for its artists, hydrangeas, and tranquility, all set within a jungle wonderland.

Almost everyone in the Village is an artist; if not an artist, they probably work in the Park. If not that, they probably run a bed-and-breakfast or vacation rental; there are almost three hundred in a storybook village with the population of only 2231! One thing is for sure, everyone who lives here loves it and appreciates and protects this very special and sacred environment. For you folks who would like to share in the flavor of the Village, if for a day or longer, you will find here wonderful tidbits of information to make your visit forever memorable.

*This might be a good place for a little pedantic spelling lesson. You may have seen the word *Hawaii* and the word *Hawai'i*, this latter spelled with what is called an 'okina, a consonant letter in many Polynesian languages. Are they interchangeable? No! *Hawaii* refers to the state of Hawaii, while *Hawai'i* refers to the Big Island of Hawaii. In 1959, our Statehood Act used the spelling "Hawaii" and an act of Congress would be required to change the name of the state to "Hawai'i". Just in case you ever wonder!

The Park Now!
Post Eruption 2018!

Wow! What just happened? Here I (we) are, living in Paradise, and suddenly my (our) world is completely rocked! Literally! Changed in a twinkling!

We just experienced the historical Kilauea eruption of 2018!

But Yippie Ki-Yay! We're still here! Volcano Village is still here! And Hawai'i Volcanoes National Park has reopened! Life in Paradise goes on!

My guide to the Park and its environs has been a staple handbook since 2012 for many who have wanted to plan their trip to Kilauea *before* they come so that they can get the most out of it! With the recent *huge* eruptive events of the volcano, the Park has changed immensely. With 62 collapse events between May and August 2018, many places in the Park have been rendered dangerous by rockfalls, sinkholes, and cracked and fractured trails. Kilauea Caldera subsided 500 meters!!! That's more than three times its previous depth. Halema'uma'u is unrecognizable—the lava lake disappeared from sight but is reappearing again! Jaggar Museum and Hawaiian Volcano Observatory have had to relocate, and their structures perched precariously on the edge of the caldera have been abandoned. Roads have been destroyed or are impassable. Some areas in the Park have not yet been ascertained safe; they are being reopened carefully and methodically. The Park plans to reopen sections as they are deemed safe, while, if necessary, they may have to close some areas.

This presented a dilemma for me as far as revising my guidebook. After thinking about it a lot, I decided to leave my guide as it was, and instead of deleting information about areas that may not yet be open again, I will give additional information as updates change. And, because the eruption was so fascinating on many levels (indeed, it was a first as far as volcanologists observing the actual subsidence of a volcanic caldera), I have chronicled a day by day chronicle of events as they happened in the final chapter of this guide. By doing so, I hope you too can relive the excitement our little ole drive-in volcano gave us for three whole months (without the stress!)

*

My Favorite Places

Here it is—a list of my favorite places! This guide will take you to all these extraordinary places, and more. However, due to the extraordinary damage to the Park environs from the 2018 eruption, some of these places are closed. The Park plans to reopen them section by section, as they are deemed safe. Each subsection of this guide indicates whether an area is open or closed at present.

Remember, not all of these wonderful places are open yet, and some will not reopen. You can also check here at the National Park Service page for up to date info on closures of different areas, as daily closures can occur due to weather, traffic, air quality, repairs and even because the nene birds are nesting!

Basic Information - Hawai'i Volcanoes National Park (U.S. National Park (nps.gov) Service)

Currently closed indefinitely are:

Crater Rim Drive beyond Uēkahuna (site of Jaggar Museum and the old Volcano Observatory) and Jaggar Museum

My Favorite Places

Ainahou Ranch
Chain of Craters Road
Devastation Trail and Desolation Peak
Halema'uma'u Trail
Hilina Pali Trail
Holei Sea Arch
Keonehelelei—"The Falling Sands" Also called Ka'u
 Desert Footprints or sometimes just "Footprints"
Kilauea Caldera
Kilauea Iki Caldera Overlook and Trail
Devil's Throat
Kipukapuaulu (Bird Park)
Mauna Ulu (Growing Mountain)
Nahuku Crater and Thurston Lava Tube
Namakanipaio (The Conflicting Winds)
Kilauea Overlook and Uēkahuna Bluff
Napau Trail (The Endings)
'Ola'a Rainforest
Place of the Guardians (Pele's Playground)
Pu'u Huluhulu (Shaggy Hill)
Puapo'o (Cock's Comb Cave, Wild Cave)
Pu'upua'i Overlook
Pu'uloa Petroglyphs
Wahinekapu (Steaming Bluff) called Steam Vents
Ha'kulamanu – called Sulphur Banks
'Iliahi Trail (Sandalwood Trail)
The Enchanted Forest
The Mauna Loa Strip Road
Tree Molds
Volcano Art Gallery

***

I know you're eager to know all about the current eruption, which began in 2021, so let's begin with everything you need to know to view this spectacular event!

Eruption 2021! Ongoing!

You're in luck! An immense lava lake is in the making, and lava is visible from many overlooks within th park. The current eruption began September 29, 2021, just four months after the 2018 eruption was officially declared ended. On that day, the Volcano Observatory detected a fissure eruption in Halema'uma'u crater in the Kilauea summit caldera (*Kaluapele* is the Hawaiian name, which means "the pit of Pele"). Since then it has erupted steadily except for brief pauses lasting as long as three days. Nothing is predictable! Therefore, changes can occur literally minute by minute! You just have to be there when it happens!

It all began at 3:30 p.m. September 29 when three fissures opened up in an east wall in Halema'uma'u and began to flow over the previous lava lake created in 2018. About an hour later, another fissure opened up on the west wall. Eighty-five thousand tones of sulfur dioxide emissions were generated that first day. Lava was only slightly visible from the crater, but could be seen from the air.

By October 1, the lava lake had risen 89 feet and was about 134 acres in area. The fountain heights on October 2 were bursting to 55-66 yards. In the next days, lava continued fountaining and pouring into the lake. On October 10, a magnitude 6.2 earthquake hit offshore southwest of the island, causing some consternation and fear among Volcano residents who had just gone through the destruction of the 2018 eruption, but it had no observable effect on Kilauea volcano except for a few small rock falls.

On October 24, the lava lake was observable for the first time from the rim of the crater at Kilauea Overlook. On December 4, the rate of lava decreased sharply, possibly marking a pause in the eruption, and a portion of the vent cone collapsed.

On December 6, the eruption resumed again!

And on December 14, there was a slight pause, and then the eruption continued.

Current conditions, closures and daily updates from the Park can be had here: Kīlauea Volcano Eruption Update - Hawai'i Volcanoes National Park (U.S. National Park Service) (nps.gov)

and from the Geological Survey here:

Volcano Watch — A new eruption in Halema'uma'u | U.S. Geological Survey (usgs.gov)

Most residents of Volcano visit the eruption site often, and we keep one another in the loop. It's the Volcano version of the Coconut Wireless. Thus, we know within a few hours, if not minutes. of the latest developments of the eruption. Hearing that an event has occurred, such as an increase in lava flow, or an inflation event, might trigger our fears, or more often, our excitement, or conversely, hearing that lava output has decreased, might appease them. An earthquake big enough to be felt might set us on alert, because most of us have lived through eruptions that were life changing.

But one thing for sure, those of us who choose to live here, love our volcano. We hope you will too!

Now, how to best see the stupendous sight of earth giving birth?

Viewing the Eruption

The outstanding feature of the current eruption is the lava lake, with molten lava cascading into the lower pit of the main lava lake. Lava is plunging underneath the crater floor, causing the crater floor to rise. More than 20 billion gallons of lave have filled Halema'uma'u crater since the beginning of the eruption. And you are going to see this amazing spectacle!

The best viewing is of course at night! The Park is currently thronged with visitors; most want to view the eruption at its best, so **if possible, plan to go between the hours of 12 a.m. and daylight.** Of course, for most people that's not feasible, but just to let you know, the parking lots can get full between 4 p. m. and 8 p. m. Go at 9 p. m. and you're good!

You'll witness a captivating red glow coming from the volcanic plume arising from the crater, and depending on conditions, be mesmerized by the stream of blazing red lava pouring into the molten lava lake below. If you do go at night, **dress warmly**—the night wind can be uncomfortably cold. Rain is often a possibility, so be prepared with **rain gear**. Sneakers are fine, but forego open-toed shoes. Also, a **flashlight is necessary**. If possible, binoculars are a real plus! Because of the crowds, please take turns at the edge of the caldera where the best views are to be had. People are generally polite so no need to push and shove and cause someone to go over the edge and get roasted (just kidding!). There is a Port-a-Potty at the parking lot, and rangers are there in case there are any problems, or if you have questions. If you do go during peak viewing times in the early evening, you may need to wait for a parking place, but generally it's not long, maybe 20 minutes or so.

If you go during the day, the fiery stream of lava will hardly be visible, but you will be able to see the volcanic plume of gas and steam rising like a beautiful wraith out of Halema'uma'u. Rain and fog, which are likely to occur, may further obscure the eruption view itself, but the eerie landscape will still make an indelible memory—I actually love the foggy and misty days out there. The lava fountaining itself is only visible from the south caldera rim near Keanakako'i Overlook, which I will explain below. So, if you want to avoid crowds and traffic, go during the day. I go often during the day and I am the only one out there! Or if can, do both—go during the day and the night!

Stay on the trails! Do not go wandering off-trail— cracks and cliff edges can be dangerous, and falling into one or over one can be fatal! Please drive slowly. It's tempting to take the curves going down hill especially like a roller coaster, but...one cross over the white line by another car or a bicyclist in the road can be tragic. Take your time and enjoy everything, including the drive.

Be aware that the Park is a sacred place for the native Hawaiians, *the* most sacred place. You may witness some cultural events taking place, including hula and chanting. Be respectful, don't gawk, and be quiet.

During this time of Covid, even though you are outdoors, please maintain social distancing of six feet, and mask up if there is a crowd. Also, those with heart and respiratory problems, elderly persons, infants and young children and pregnant women should be cautious— volcanic gasses are toxic.

OK! Cautions taken, so **where do you go to see this mighty sight?**

This is where planning your itinerary ahead of time is really helpful! Also, as you go through the Park gate, you will be handed a map. You can also download the Park app here: The NPS App - Digital (U.S. National Park Service)

There are five main viewing sites.

The very best is the Keanakako'i Overlook. There are two places to park, as I will explain. The closest will involve a two-mile walk along the paved road, the second will involve a three-mile walk.

To get to Keanakako'i, turn left **immediately** after going through the Park gate. You have to look sharp to make the turn as you come directly out of the Park gate. From there, a short drive of a minute will take you to a stop sign where you will turn left. This is Crater Rim Drive. Follow it three miles as it winds down, down, down and you will come to the intersection of Chain of Craters Road. You can't miss it. You will see a barricade across from the stop sign.

For the closest parking, t**urn right into the Devastation Trail parking lot. Walk the short distance back after parking to the barricade** and Port-a-Potties and take a right on Old Crater Rim Drive. You'll can't miss it. The paved road is closed to traffic except for the rangers. Most likely you will see other pedestrians and some rangers. A little more than a one-mile walk will take you to the best views of the lava fountains and the lava lake, so all in all, **this is about a two-mile walking trip,** as I said.

If it's clear, and night time, you will enjoy an unforgettable walk out under the stars, if it's clear. If it's not, you will still enjoy the silence and ambiance. If it's daytime, you will enjoy unforgettable views of expansive volcanic vistas, as well as the beautiful trees and plants, and you may see the Nene geese. Don't pick their beautiful red berries, please.

The view into the caldera is of the lava plunging into a smaller pit, and lava fountaining as much as 30 feet from the lava lake roiling below.

While you're at Keanakako'i Overlook, take a look at the **Keanakako'i Crater,** across the street from the eruption sight. You can't see much at night but you can get a good look during the day. "Keanakako'i" means "cave of the adzes" and was a special place were the kahuna kako'i, carving experts, obtained superior and rare basaltic rock for making their ko'i, their adze heads, used for carving canoes and houses and weapons. It probably formed in the 1400's. Lava overtook it in 1877 and 1974, and today it is only 115 deep. You can imagine the warriors of old working the crater.

Take your time walking back to the parking lot and enjoy the walk along the road free from traffic. Back in the day, before the volcanic plume started going off in 2009 and the park closed half of the road because of toxic gasses, I used to ride my back completely around the almost 13 mile Crater Rim Drive, when the complete road was open. I miss it! It was a world class bike ride.

A second possibility, especially if the parking lot at Devastation Trail just mentioned is full, or you want a little more exercise and volcanic experience, is to park at the **Pu'upua'i Overlook on Chain of Craters Road, before the Devastation Trail parking lot.** You'll see it on your right as you wind down Crater Rim Drive after passing Thurston lava tube before the Devastation Trail parking lot—**it's the first road branching off you'll see, and will be on the right.** This is a great place to park, because fewer people will park there. First, if it is daytime, take a minute or more to enjoy the view of the overlook down into Kilauea Iki. You can then walk most of the way on a sidewalk that will meet up to the Devastation Trail parking lot just described. It's about a half-mile one way. This then, will make a total of **a three-mile round-trip hike to the eruption site and back**. During daytime especially, I recommend this possibility, if you like to walk, because you will see beautiful native plants and possibly enjoy native birds singing along the sidewalk trail.

Want total easy? Then the view from the Volcano House might be for you. You can park at the Kilauea

Visitor Center, walk across the street to the Volcano House, and either watch the eruption from inside the dining room, or from outside on the sidewalk. Face masks are required inside Volcano House. You can even eat at the restaurant while enjoying the eruption!

A third viewing site and with easy access is the Kilauea Overlook at Uēkahuna bluff. After entering the Park gate, continue driving straight ahead, west, for just over two miles until you see the sign "Kilauea" on your left. A very short walk will take you to a view as good as weather conditions permit—you may or may not see the lava lake below, but you will see a spectacular red glow. The view of the eruption is from a one-mile distance. If you go at night, a flashlight is a must! There is a restroom.

A fourth viewing sight is Wahinekapu, accessible from the Steam Vents parking area, which is one mile straight ahead from the Park gate, going west. Park at the Steam Vents. No restroom; again, a flashlight is a must if you go at night.

A fifth viewing area is from Kupina'i Pali Overlook (Waldron Ledge), one of the least crowded viewing areas. Want to enjoy the sight of active lave surface plates being dragged into the lower crater without a lot of talking and flashlights, etc.? Park at the Kilauea Visitor Center and cross Crater Rim Drive. Walk south on Crater Rim Trail. It's about a half-mile to the viewing site and the eruption itself is two miles-away. No restroom but this is wheel chair accessible.

As I said, conditions can change at any time. Make your first stop the Visitor Center, where you can get up-to-date information about all viewing sites, potential lethal volcanic fumes and other hazards, air quality and eruption activity.

Enjoy! There's no other place like Kilauea on Earth!

The Fascinating Geology of Volcanoes!

Are you ready? Let's begin with a quick overview of geology, ecology, flora, fauna and Hawaiian culture of this fabulous place. The more you know about the geology and eco-system of Kilauea, the more unforgettable your visit will be. The magic of nature is what it is all about!

Everyone is interested in geology these days. Why?

Even many scientists are wondering if we're going toward a new period of increased volcanic explosions and earthquakes. Millions of people even believe that increased volcanic activity is a sign of the end of the world, the Second Coming, impending visitations by extra-terrestrials, or Earth changes as predicted by the Mayan calendar!

At any rate, volcanoes are currently active in Italy, Russia, Chile, Ecuador, New Britain, Costa Rica, Santa Maria, Guatemala, and Indonesia, as well as in Hawaii. There has been growing concern about the huge "super volcano" in Yellowstone National Park.

Some scientists predict that, in the case of simultaneous major eruptions within a short period of time, it's possible that the Earth would be cooled by at least one to three degrees, as all the dust and ash in the upper atmosphere would partly shield the sun's rays and greatly disturb worldwide weather patterns. Earthquakes and volcanoes are related to the movement of the Earth's plates, called plate tectonics, causing changes in density and pressure, which are correlated to volcanic activity. Large earthquakes can trigger volcanic eruptions, and magma movement can cause tremors.

Recent natural disasters, such as the huge earthquake and tsunami in Japan, have impressed everyone that Earth changes affect us all. And the magnitude of these disasters has reminded us that humans are powerless when confronted by these colossal forces of Mother Nature. These huge geological events have made us curious about our planet again.

Hawai'i Volcanoes National Park offers the visitor a look at two of the world's most active volcanoes: Kilauea and Mauna Loa.

More than 4,000 feet high and still growing, Kilauea abuts the southeastern slope of the older and much larger Mauna Loa, or "Long Mountain." Mauna Loa towers some 13,679 feet above the sea, making it the tallest mountain in the world, and the second tallest in the solar system (Mars has the honor of the highest mountain). Yes, it's true. Measured from its base 18,000 feet below sea level, Mauna Loa exceeds Mount Everest in height.

Hawai'i Volcanoes National Park stretches from sea level to Mauna Loa's summit. Seven ecological zones exist within Hawai'i Volcanoes National Park. Each zone consists of distinct plant and animal communities. Kilauea's caldera is surrounded by three zones: rainforest on the east, upland forests and woodlands on the northwest, and mid-elevation woodlands to the south.

Beyond the end of the road to Mauna Loa lies Mauna Loa's wilderness area, where hikers encounter freezing nights and jagged lava trails amid volcanic wonders: stark lava twisted into black licorice shapes, cinder cones, gaping pits.

Kilauea, however, provides easy access to a greater variety of scenery and cultural sites. In fact, it is often called the "drive-in" volcano. On the slopes of Kilauea, whose name means "much spewing," lush green rainforests border barren, recent lava flows.

We're lucky!

Why?

Because for all its activity, and Kilauea has been continuously active now since 1983, Kilauea is a relatively "safe" volcano, at least as compared to other active volcanoes. Not that it hasn't created a path of devastation! It has destroyed more than 181 houses, a visitor center in the Park as well as important archaeological sites, and its lava flows have enveloped roads and covered the famed Kalapana Black Sand Beach.

But it is considered "safe" and is the most visited volcano in the world because of the *type* of volcano it is; it is what is called a "shield" volcano. **The Hawaiian Islands are all formed by shield volcanoes.**

The form of a volcano is determined by the ingredients of the erupting magma. Their shapes are determined by the explosivity of the eruptions and the amount of water in the magma. Shield volcanoes are low and broad, with the entire summit region flattened or depressed. They have rift zones: two to four cracks radiating from the summit. Think *huge* cracks! Not the kind you can jump over!

Shield volcanoes are almost exclusively basalt, a type of lava that is very fluid when erupted. For this reason, these volcanoes are not steep-sided, but shaped like a warrior's shield; hence the name. Eruptions at shield volcanoes are only explosive if water somehow gets into the vent; otherwise, they are characterized by low-explosive fountaining that forms cinder cones and spatter cones at the vent. **Shield volcanoes are the result of high magma supply rates; the lava is hot and little changed from the time it was generated.** Shield volcanoes are the common product of *hotspot* volcanism. More on hotspots in a moment.

On the other hand, "subduction-zone strato" volcanoes are tall and steep, with limited summit depression and no rift zones. Subduction-strato volcanoes comprise the largest percentage, almost 60%, of the Earth's volcanoes, and are characterized by eruptions of andesite and dacite—lavas that are cooler and more viscous than basalt. These more viscous lavas allow gas pressures to build up to high levels; these volcanoes are characterized by violent, explosive eruptions. The lava at strato volcanoes barely flows, instead piling up in the vent to form volcanic domes. The magma supply rates to strato volcanoes are lower. This is the cause of the cooler magma and the reason for the usually long repose periods between eruptions. Examples of strato volcanoes include Mt. St. Helens, Mt. Rainier, Pinatubo, Mt. Fuji, Merapi, Galeras, Cotopaxi, and others.

In other words, what this means is that, in general, shield volcanoes, like Hawaii's volcanoes, not being accompanied by pyroclastic material, such as rocks and gasses of up to 1830 degrees Fahrenheit, moving at speeds of over 100-450 miles per hour, are relatively safe for us to explore!

This does not mean, however, that shield volcanoes never have explosive episodes. In fact, in 1959, Kilauea Iki caldera, *one of the must-see sights* on your visit, erupted violently in fountains 1900 feet tall! The good news is, however, that it gave plenty of warning, preceding its violent outburst by swarms of earthquakes beginning three months in advance of its November 14th eruption.

Speaking of earthquakes, just to let you know, a number of earthquakes occur daily in the Kilauea area. Most of the time, these are below the threshold of perception. But, if you decide to spend a night in Volcano Village, and if you are extremely sensitive, as I am, you may feel the earth trembling as you lay in bed at night. And if you are extremely sensitive, you may be interested to know that that faint rumble that you are not sure if you hear or feel, as you lie quietly in bed at night in the Village, may be coming from the roiling magma just one to four miles beneath the summit!

Though the chance of being caught in an explosive eruption in the Park is remote, there are very real dangers, and an entire section of this guide will be devoted to possible hazards and cautionary measures. But as I am writing now of fire and brimstone, this would be a good

19

place to mention that, though Kilauea is often called the "drive-in" volcano, injuries and deaths do happen. In 1993, my good friend, photographer Prem Nagar, had a fiery but surely quick death when a small earthquake caused the newly formed lava shelf on which he had ventured for up-close photos, to drop into the sea, heated beyond boiling by the river of molten lava flowing into it. He was never recovered. So, for all the Park's beauty, please remember, you are not in Disneyland!

Pertinent geological facts relating to specific sites will be discussed below, but here is some more fascinating information relating to the way new earth is formed by the volcanoes here in Hawaii.

You may not know but the Hawaiian Islands are only part of a long continuous chain of islands that stretches northwest of Kauai 1900 miles to Midway Island and the Kure atoll and beyond. **The Hawaiian Island chain is one of the largest and most striking features on the surface of planet Earth, yet it is not related to any of the major types of plate boundaries.** The chain consists not only of the main Hawaiian Islands and adjacent French Frigate shoals, but also the Emperor Seamounts, a submarine range that runs northward to the Aleutian subduction zone where it disappears. This continuous line of volcanoes represents anomalous (unusual) lava production and by implication, a zone of excess heat in the underlying mantle. In the early 1960's, the term "hotspot" was coined for regions like Hawaii where anomalous heat was recognized, though the origin of such regions remains a geological mystery.

What exactly is a hotspot? Think of a Krispy Kreme machine! Geologists believe that a huge column of up-welling lava, known as a "plume," lies at a fixed position under the Pacific Plate. As the ocean floor moves over this "hot spot" at about five inches a year, the up-welling lava creates a steady succession of new volcanoes that migrate along with the plate.

The Hawaiian-Emperor chain is the most famous and well studied of the hot spots that dot our planet. The youngest islands lie to the southeast, with the Big Island being the newest. The islands and seamounts become progressively older towards the northwest, bending sharply toward the north about halfway along its length. About 30-40 million years ago, something caused the direction of plate movement to change from almost due north to northwest, resulting in the Hawaii-Emperor Bend. A huge meteor strike, perhaps? No one knows.

The oldest seamounts are found at the northwest end of the trench, poised to plunge beneath the Aleutian volcanic arc. Picture a conveyor belt! The oldest volcanoes yet to be consumed are 70 million years old, having erupted at about the time that the last dinosaur died. Now these old volcanoes are dying. In other words, the hot spot has channeled magma up since at least the end of the dinosaur age. How many other volcanoes have already been subsumed we have no way of knowing.

The farther the other islands in the chain are from Hawaii, the greater their age. About 150 miles to the northwest is Oahu, which burst out of the sea about 3.5 million years ago. Midway, one of the oldest islands in the chain, was formed between 15 and 25 million years ago.

All in all, there are about 80 volcanoes from here to Alaska; that means on average about one volcano was made every one million years. As these volcanoes float off the hot spot, and move toward the Aleutians, they begin to sink. Why? Due to their weight, as well as factors of erosion by wind and water, gradually, as they age, where once they were mighty mountains, they become nothing more than coral reefs. They sink approximately 0.8 inches per 1000 years.

The Hawaiian archipelago consists of eight high islands, which means islands that have their highest elevation greater than a few hundred meters. These eight comprise 99% of the chain's emergent land area, land

21

above the sea. These and the Northwestern Hawaiian Islands form a chain about 1500 miles long, with no continent closer than 2000 miles. It is the most isolated major group of islands on Earth.

More about the mysterious hotspots. There are about 100 hotspots on the planet, but the total amount of lava produced by these is relatively slight, less than 1% of the volcanic material extruded worldwide. It has, interestingly, a different chemical composition than lava produced from the sea floor or subduction zones, the other two ways lava is produced. Hotspot magma is basalt. It contains less silicon as well as more iron and magnesium than does andesite. Andesite is continental igneous rock, containing high amounts of silicon, calcium, sodium and potassium, with low amounts of iron and magnesium.

To refresh your memory from fourth grade science, molten rock, when still under the Earth, is called *magma.* When it rises to the surface, it is called *lava.*

You may also recall from your fourth grade science class that there are three layers of the Earth—the core, the mantle, and the crust. The core is the innermost portion, and is believed to be solid in the center and molten on its outer layer, with a temperature of up to 7000 Celsius. The mantle surrounds the core, heated to extremely high temperatures by the core. It is probably not liquid, but fluid enough to deform and flow very slowly. The crust is the very thin outer layer, consisting of the rigid rock of the seafloors and the continents.

Molten rock, magma, is somehow, not exactly known how, drawn or pushed up the hotspot to the surface, where it becomes a "seamount." As it grows and finally breaks the surface, it becomes an "island." The five volcanoes of the Big Island are sort of fused together to form what we call Hawai'i Island.

These five connected volcanic mountains were built by a lava plume rising from the mantle. They are Mauna Loa, Kilauea, Mauna Kea, Hualalai, and Kohala. Kilauea, the world's most active volcano, is still rumbling because the island has yet to drift completely off the hot spot.

Kohala is the oldest of Hawaii's sub-aerial volcanoes, about 430,000 years old. It is currently about 1670 meters above sea level, a loss of 1000 meters from its highest elevation, because it is already beginning to erode. It is considered extinct; it has not erupted for 60,000 years.

Mauna Kea is a dormant volcano and last erupted about 4500 years ago. It will probably erupt again some day. Interestingly, **Mauna Kea is the only volcano in the Hawaiian chain known to have been glaciated.** About 15,000 years ago, a glacier descended to about the 11,000 feet level and melted. Glacial ice resulted in a type of rock that was highly sought after by the ancient Hawaiians for adzes, because it is fine-grained and vesicle free, making it less likely to shatter. Mauna Loa was high enough to have had glaciers, but if glacial deposits formed, they have been buried by later flows.

Hualalai is the third most active volcano in Hawaii, and last erupted in 1801. It is expected to erupt again within the next 100 years.

Did you fly in via the Kona airport? That airport, and the surrounding real estate, some of the priciest in the world, are built upon that 1801 lava flow. Flows from Hualalai will reach the sea in less than a day. If and when Hualalai erupts again, there's a lot of Kailua-Kona in the way!

Mauna Loa, the largest mountain on Earth, covers 51% of the Big Island. Since 1850, is has erupted on average every 7-10 years. It last erupted in 1984. You can see it is long overdue; it may erupt again at any time. Mauna Loa probably emerged from the sea 400,000 years, and has been erupting for 700,000 years.

Kilauea is the star, however. Beloved and feared as the home of the fire goddess Pele, Halema'uma'u Crater, the center of Kilauea volcano, has been the source of countless Hawaiian legends. Kilauea, the youngster of the

Hawaii volcanoes, first erupted between 300,000 and 600,000 years ago. That hotspot mentioned earlier is directly underneath Kilauea, perhaps as deep as 2000 miles into the mantle of the planet. The caldera was the site of nearly continuous activity during the 19th century and the early part of this century.

Since 1952, Kilauea has erupted 34 times, and since January 1983, eruptive activity has been continuous along the east rift zone. Currently, there is a lava lake within Halema'uma'u that rises and falls with the inflation and deflation of the lava beneath its summit, often exposing its red-hot interior. More on this later!

Note that in the paragraph about Kohala volcano the term *subaerial volcano* was used. That means a growing volcano has added enough mass and height to end frequent contact with water, thereby becoming less explosive.

There actually is **an older volcano that formed Hawai'i Island, Mahukona**.

Mahukona is submerged on the northwestern flank of Island. Now it is a drowned coral reef at about 3,770 feet below sea level. A major break in slope at about 4,400 feet below sea level represents its old shorelines. The summit of this shield volcano was once 800 feet above sea level. The main shield-building stage of volcanism ended about 470,000 years ago. The summit subsided below sea level between 435,000 and 365,000 years ago. This makes Mahukona the granddaddy volcano of Hawai'i Island.

And what's that about a baby volcano? Are we expecting?

Yes!

Though Kilauea is growing and will continue to grow throughout human history, it is not the baby volcano. That distinction goes to... **Lo'ihi**. Still technically a *seamount* rather than a volcano, Lo'ihi is the youngest volcano of the Hawaiian chain, lying about 35 km off the SE coast of the island of Hawai'i. Nine hundred and fifty meters below sea level, this baby already has a caldera.

Lo'ihi began forming around 400,000 years ago, and will emerge above the sea about 10,000 to 100,000 years from now. It now stands more than 3,000 meters above the seafloor, making it taller than Mt. St. Helens before its 1980 eruption. If you're interested in buying prime ocean front real estate, for only $39.95, you can buy a parcel of Lo'ihi Seaview Estates now. Just Google it if you're interested!

We'll have more site-specific geology later on!

Epic Ecology

Barren rocks in vast ocean waters, thousands of miles from the nearest land! How did the incredible diversity of life ever reach Hawaii shores?

Hawaii is 2551 miles from Los Angeles, 3850 miles from Japan, and 5280 miles from the Philippines, but insects and spiders and the seeds of plants reached the islands by wind or in the digestive tracts of birds or stuck to birds blown far off course. Sea currents carried salt-resistant seeds to these far shores, and perhaps some plants and animals floated here merely by chance, clinging to floating flotsam and jetsam.

Who can recount the heroic struggle of some desperate creature, hanging on for dear life?

What were the odds of life reaching these shores? And surviving?

It is estimated that a plant or animal colonized Hawaii at the rate of one every 70,000 years. Over the past 70 million years, before the arrival of humans, few arrived; fewer survived.

The fortunate species that did make it to these islands evolved over time into new forms and species, and adapted to a life with an absence of predators and competitors. Because of this, they no longer depended upon highly evolved defense mechanisms. Native plants evolved in the absence of mammalian plant eaters and lost ancestral defenses against predation such as thorny and poisonous foliage, bitter barks, and roots resistant to trampling. Plants did not need to evolve thorns or poisons for their protection; birds did not necessarily need wings!

More than 90% percent of the native flora and fauna of Hawaii is **endemic, which means found nowhere else on our planet.** From perhaps 20 original ancestors, the Island's 100 endemic birds evolved! Of Hawaii's native angiosperms (flowering plants) comprising some 1400 species, more than 96 percent are endemic, the rest are indigenous. Ten thousand spider and insect species evolved from only 350 to 400 ancestors! Native ferns comprise about 170 species, with around 65 percent endemic. Mosses and liverworts are similar to ferns in these statistics. The Islands became home to only two endemic mammals, the Hawaiian monk seal and the hoary bat.

Most of these plants and animals lived together in a delicious harmony of co-existence, a Garden of Eden. There were no reptiles or amphibians. Hawaii was originally a paradise—no ants, mosquitoes, cockroaches, scorpions or large venomous centipedes. No snakes!

Where did these colonizers come from?

Only about 18% have affinities with North American species. The remainder came from Malaysia, Australia, New Zealand, southern South America and southeast Asia.

A Garden of Eden.

Then humans came. Predators.

The ancient Hawaiians brought a cornucopia of 26 plants and the pig, the dog, the rat. They burned the lands along the seacoasts for their agriculture. They hunted and exterminated many birds including the flightless giant birds, which some Hawaiian legends describe as big as a man! Before Captain Cook arrived, more than 35 endemic Hawaiian land birds had already become extinct.

But when western man hit these shores, the real destruction of this Garden of Eden began, and in earnest. Not intentionally, of course. Cattle, goats, cats, mongooses, and pigs and rats more than twice the size of the Polynesian predators were set free. So were diseases. So were 10,000 alien plants.

The delicate plants and animals of the Garden, who had evolved no protection because they needed none, were gobbled up, trampled upon, and exterminated at a rate tragically unbelievable. This was long before the days of the science of ecology, and the development in humans of

27

an ecological conscience. Over 1,000 plants and animals have disappeared from the Garden since human colonization, and currently Hawaii has 317 threatened and endangered plant and animal species. *The bell is tolling for Hawaiian nature.* One-third of the US roster of endangered species is Hawaiian species. One-half, 50%, of native insects, have disappeared forever.

Today, Hawaii is in the death throes of a full-scale alien invasion. Millions of tourists and the cargo-holds of ships and jetliners offer an easy road to paradise for hitchhiking alien plants, animals, and insects. Bird-eating snakes hide invidiously in the wheel wells of airplanes arriving from Guam. Visitors intentionally sneak in alien animals and plants as well; they unintentionally bring diseases. Seeds from exotic ornamental plants imported by well-meaning home gardeners escape from backyards to sprout and proliferate in dry forestland already more than decimated by human habitation.

There are about 150 distinctive ecosystems in the Hawaiian Islands. These ecosystems are so distinct that the Hawaiian Islands constitute a unique global bio-region. These ecosystems include tropical dry forests, sub-alpine grasslands, snowy alpine deserts, brackish anchialine pools, subterranean lava tube systems with eyeless creatures, and windswept coastal dunes. You name it; the islands have it.

Some native ecosystems have been very hard hit. Over 90% of Hawaiian lowland dry forests have been lost to agriculture, development, fire, or weed invasions. Other ecosystems have been relatively less impacted. Alpine deserts on the summit of Mauna Loa, for example, are very much as they were before humans came. But half of the 150 ecosystem types are in danger, imperiled by human-related alterations in the ecosystem. Most of the loss has occurred along the coasts and in the lowlands, where the majority of human habitation exists today, but the rainforests are greatly imperiled.

Hawaii is the Extinction Capital of the World. Over 75% of the United States extinctions have occurred here. We are also known as "The Endangered Species Capital of the World" with over 25% of the United States endangered species located in Hawaii. Yet, Hawaii has only 0.2% of the land area in the country!

Many more pests that are injurious now threaten to invade Hawaii and wreak further damage. The brown tree snake alone could forever change the character of our islands. Hawaii's future well being depends upon stopping and containing the influx of new pests. It is estimated that **new species are being introduced to Hawaii at a rate that is 2 million times more rapid than the natural rate!**

An amazing array of endemic plants and animals, which occur nowhere else on Earth, call the rainforest home. Soaring over forests of koa and 'ohi'a, endangered Hawaiian hawks search for prey among exotic vines where spectacular native tree snails hide. Forest birds such as the Hawaiian crow and Hawaiian thrush have no other habitat in which to live, except, tragically, in cages. Ditto for native honeycreepers, birds that have evolved diverse bill structures for feeding on particular plants in mesic and wet forests. Several marvelous carnivorous caterpillars are endemic to Hawaii. These fantastic creatures mimic twigs and snatch prey that mistakenly comes too close; others perch on tree trunks, or wait on ferns and leaves. When triggered by touch, these caterpillars pounce on their unsuspecting prey.

Saving these unique and precious remaining native species and habitats is now a race against time.

Do you know—*the tropical rainforests are the single greatest terrestrial source of air that we breathe?* Often described as the Earth's lungs, the tropical rainforests take in vast quantities of carbon dioxide, a poisonous gas that mammals exhale, and through the process of photosynthesis, convert it into clean, breathable air.

29

Do you know that *while the tropical rainforests cover just 2% of the Earth's land surface, they are home to two-thirds of all the living species on the planet?*

Do you know that *nearly half the medicinal compounds we use every day come from plants endemic to the tropical rainforest?* Within some of the rainforest lava caves of Hawaii, for example, there exist bacteria that may be possible cures for cancer.

For all our calculations, no one can predict what will happen to Island bio-diversity in the future, but perhaps clues can be found in the fiery nature of Hawaii itself. Every day, as fresh lava flows into the ocean, new land is formed—land that will, in time, become new habitat for Hawaiian plants and animals, both native and invasive. Life is change. Just as the geography of Hawaii is always changing, so will the shape of life on these wonderful Islands.

One thing is certain. Visitors to Hawaii are very blessed to experience this treasure as it is now.

Fantastic Flora and Fauna

Native species of plants and animals are of two groups, endemic and indigenous. *Endemic* species are only found in Hawaii; they evolved here and are now distinct species from plants and animals elsewhere in the world. *Indigenous* species are found here and elsewhere; they may have evolved here or elsewhere. Both indigenous and endemic species arrived without human help.

Hawai'i Volcanoes National Park has among the highest number, 54, of threatened and endangered plants and animals in the National Park System, mostly due to non-native species. The National Park Service is working aggressively to eradicate them.

Kilauea rainforest is unlike the other rainforests in the world in that, instead of many tree species, only one or two dominate the forest. The dominate canopy tree here are the koa, and the beautiful red-blossomed 'ohi'a lehua, the subject of many myths and legends of Hawaii. The second canopy layer is composed of 'olapa. Understory trees are kawa'u, kolea, pilo, olomea, mamaki, and opuhe. Tree ferns, called hapu'u, the largest ferns in the world, are characteristic of Hawai'i Island rainforests; they occur much less frequently, if at all, on the older islands.

The bio-diversity of Kilauea rainforest occurs in its under-story and ground cover. Ferns are paramount, with many, many species, ranging from delicate and lacy, some even only one cell thick, to stout-trunked and stiff-textured. There are native peperomias, endemic hydrangeas, giant African violet relatives, as well as succulents of the lobelia family. There are few vines.

One feature of Hawaii rainforests is the epiphytes, plants that grow on tree trunks and branches of host plants. These epiphytes don't feed off their host plants; they live in harmony. A great example of a host pant is the hapu'u. You will often see myriad numbers of other plants growing on their trunks; these hapu'u are called "nurse logs." There is also an abundance of mosses and liverworts in these rainforests.

Birds that you are likely to see and hear include the 'oma'o, which has among its calls a "police whistle," and the apapane, the beautiful, brilliant red bird that flits among the same-colored lehua blossoms. Frequently you may also see the kalij pheasant, a non-native bird with a sweet, gurgling cry.

Other interesting animals include the predaceous caterpillar mentioned above, an inchworm "dragon" that captures prey by using sticks and leaf edges to perch upon and seize their unwary victims.

Dislike spiders? One arachnid might make you smile! It's the Happy-face Spider, a translucent, yellow-bodied guy or gal with red and black markings, who wears a smiley face on his or her back. These creatures live underneath leaves of plants. Interestingly, some of the spiders here may form new species within the time of a human lifespan, they evolve so quickly.

Entire biosystems may have their own speciated plants and animals. A single cave or pit crater may have a completely different bio-system from any other on the Island. A species of spider in one lava cave may be unable to reproduce with its cousin in a lava tube just a half-mile away.

One creature to avoid is the wild pig. These guys can get rough if cornered. Especially a sow with piglets should be avoided. Pigs can run fast! Don't count on outrunning a pig!

That strange creature that looks like a little locomotive darting across the road or through the forest is a mongoose. Brought here to control rats, it has wiped out entire bird populations. Unfortunately, as it turned out, rats are nocturnal and mongooses (plural of mongoose!) are diurnal. They rarely meet. Unfortunately.

Myth, Legend and Culture

According to Hawaiian myths, Kilauea's violent eruptions are caused by Pele, the beautiful, hotheaded Goddess of Fire, during her frequent fits of temper. Pele historically was both revered and feared; her immense power and many adventures figure prominently in ancient Hawaiian songs and chants. Stamping her feet, she causes earthquakes. By digging with the pa'oe, her magic stick, she causes volcanic eruptions and fiery devastation.

Legend describes the long and bitter quarrel between Pele and her older sister Namakaokahai that led to the creation of the chain of volcanoes that form the Islands. Pele was seeking fire, and dug pits in succession on the islands of Kauai, Oahu, Molokai, and Maui as her sister pursued her from their homeland island far to the south. At Maui, however, Namakaokahai finally caught up with her, killed her, and scattered her bones in the sea.

Pele returned, however, as an eruptive cloud over the still-active volcanoes on the Big Island of Hawai'i. Here she dug a pit, the volcanic caldera known as Kilauea, and at last made her home in smoking Halema'uma'u Crater. As always, she's given to anger, and vents her rage by spitting out rivers of hot lava to swallow up those who displease her. To placate her ire, islanders toss sacrifices into the crater, including bottles of rum! More than once, an advancing flow of lava has stopped just short of a vulnerable village soon after such a sacrifice.

Go figure!

Stories about Pele are endless. Local Hawaiians as well as *haoles*, as "newcomers" to the Islands are called, give her credence and respect. You will probably see offerings of ti leaves and flower leis left throughout the Park for the Madam. Besides appearing as a beautiful, tempestuous redhead, she is said sometimes to go about disguised as an old crone, sometimes with a little white dog. In this guise, she tests mortals' kindness to her.

I myself have a friend, whom I consider responsible and truthful, who said that one rainy night, out of pity, she stopped her car to offer one such old woman a ride. The woman told her she was Pele. She did not have her white dog with her.

According to King Kalakaua, who ruled Hawaii from 1874-1891, there was an actual Pele clan. Driven from Samoa in the eleventh century, they made their home at Kilauea. Attacked by a hostile chief who desired to take one beautiful young Pele maiden for his lover, the Pele clan holed up in a cave, which, unfortunately, was inundated by fire and lava when the volcano erupted. Thus began the many myths of Pele.

By the way, there are still people on the Island with the last name "Pele."

How is it that Pele's home—black, smoky, and virtually barren—is cloaked in the rich greenery of the voluptuous rainforest? That's another well-known story, though there are many versions of it.

It seems that one of those smitten with her beauty was Kamapua'a, the pig demigod who could take many forms, one of which is the a'ma'u fern, one of the most prominent tree ferns of Kilauea, a fern covered with black, stiff bristles resembling those of a boar.

Kamapua'a got it into his head to woo the Madam by planting the lush green vegetation around her home while she was sleeping, much as these days a would-be suitor might leave a dozen red roses on his sweetheart's doorstep. Much to his chagrin, when Pele awoke and climbed out of her pit, she was enraged by what she saw.

She chased Kamapua'a and came close to catching him, so close that she burned his behind. The story tells us that the brilliant red a'ma'u fern frond, a form of the demigod, standing out in the sea of lush green, is a sign of the battle between Pele and Kamapua'a. These vibrant red fronds are called Ehupua'a, meaning "burnt-singed pig."

And that is how Halema'uma'u got its name, "house of the a'ma'u fern."

Another important goddess of Kilauea is Laka. She is the niece of Pele, and the goddess of the forest, the patron goddess of the hula, and sometimes she is considered the goddess of love. Also the Hawaiian goddess of plenty, the song, and the rainstorm, she is very popular and her cult includes the placing of wreaths on her sacred hula alter. If you allow yourself, you may get a fleeting glimpse of Laka in the dancing, gently swaying trees and plants of the rainforest.

Ancient Hawaiians did not live up here on Kilauea; it was too sacred and too scary! Pele might erupt at any time! Only solitary bird catchers and herb gatherers wandered the forest trails, though occasionally groups of warriors might cross the land. One such unlucky group had their footprints immortalized in the 1790 event of Keonehelelei, "the falling sands." You'll learn more about this fascinating occurrence when you read about "Footprints" later in this guide. It's a place I hope you can visit, one of my faves!

Caution!

Though Hawai'i Volcanoes National Park and the Kilauea area may seem like Disneyland, it is not. You can get lost, and never be found. Just a few years ago, one of our Village residents strolled into the forest for what she thought was to be a short walk—she was lost for two days.

The bad news is that between 1992 and 2002, there were 40 fatalities, 45 serious injuries and 53 minor injuries reported within Hawai'i Volcanoes National Park. The good news is, since, then, injuries and deaths have gone way down, due to the Park's continual efforts to educate the public on dangers.

Especially since the 2018 eruption, many areas have not been thoroughly explored and ascertained fairly safe! It could be very easy to slip through a ground crack, break through new lava, or disappear completely in a lava tube!

Never allow small children to hike alone, or run on ahead of you—they might run over a cliff! Few places within the Park have guardrails of any kind. For the most part, especially if you are not an experienced hiker, do not go off trail—there are deep holes and lava tubes, usually hidden by brush, everywhere. Do not climb down into steam vents, as one young woman did a few years ago, and was cooked. To death! And I already mentioned my friend who fell into a lava sea. Don't take chances just to get a good photo.

There is an old Hawaiian adage about walking on lava. *Keep your mouth closed and your eyes to the ground.* Good advice—which I follow.

Be aware of what we call *vog*. **Vog** is a form of air pollution that results when sulphur dioxide and other gases and particles are emitted by the Volcano. It can cause headaches, watery eyes, sore throat, and breathing difficulties. These effects are especially pronounced in people with respiratory conditions and children. Most of the time, our wonderful trade winds blow the vog over to Kona, and we here in Volcano have great air, but once in a while the wind shifts, and we get vog. There will be a sign posted at the entrance to the Park proclaiming "poor air quality" if we have a bad day. Rare, but take notice. You may have to drive around with your windows up, or even leave the area.

Hot lava releases toxic gases—hydrogen sulfide, carbon dioxide, sulphur dioxide, and hydrofluoric acid. The Plume, as we locals call it, looks like a beautiful white steam cloud, but it's acid! It can be deadly! Always hike with lots of water, and keep extra water bottles in the car.

Don't try to climb cliffs. They crumble! And of course, if lava is actively flowing, don't get too close—not only your shoes but *you* will melt!

If you hike alone, be extremely cautious. **Let someone know where you are going and when you plan to return**, even if it is the host or hostess of where you are staying. Take a GPS device if possible, or a compass. Especially observe these rules if you hike alone in the *Footprints* area or *The Place of the Guardians,* which I will describe later.

Cell phone reception is pretty good in some places in the Park, but there are lots of places where it might be non-existent, like from the bottom of a lava tube!

Take water! Have rain gear!

With that said, enjoy yourselves to the max! We have no snakes!

P. S. JFYI. The Park requires special permits for commercial use, filming, weddings and scattering of ashes. You may access the permit form here: https://www.nps.gov/havo/learn/management/upload/Sup_ Application_508.pdf

Also be aware: **drones are not allowed within the Park!**

Ready for the adventure of a lifetime?…
Let's go!

The entrance fee into the Park is $30 per car, and is good for one week. Bikes and pedestrians are $15 and motorcycles are $25 for seven days. You can get a Tri-Park annual pass for $55. Military pass? Free! And if you are 62 or older, you can get a lifetime Park pass for $80. Just a few years ago, it was only $10! Complain to your Congress!

As you drive through the Park entrance, ask for a free map! With the map, and this great guide, you can visit Kilauea's most fascinating sights.

This guide is divided into sites along Crater Rim Drive, sites along Chain of Craters Road, and sites outside of the gated entrance, including Volcano Village and the Kahuku unit in Ka'u.

Crater Rim Drive formerly was a 10.6-mile loop around Kilauea Caldera rim. (I actually measured it at 13 miles when I used to bike around it.) When Halema'uma'u began emitting her toxic plume some years ago, almost the entire southern portion of the loop was closed. After the 2018 eruption, most of the loop was closed.

Crater Rim Drive begins on the high bluff in the northeast corner of the caldera, where the Visitor Center, Volcano House Hotel and the Volcano Arts Center are located. The road leads past Kilauea Military Camp, past Kilauea Overlook, to the now closed Jaggar Museum and Volcano Observatory on Uēkahuna Bluff, and then descends down the bluff through the Southwest Rift Zone. It then ascends past Keanakako'i Crater and Thurston Lava Tube and then Kilauea Iki, and completes its loop at the Visitor Center.

Unfortunately, **a complete loop is now impossible** since the southernmost portion of the road is closed. This guide will take you necessarily therefore in two opposite directions on Crater Rim Drive, beginning from the Visitor Center.

In this guide, **we'll start first heading west from the Visitor Center (opposite the direction from the gate through which you just came)**, counterclockwise, after an essential stop at the Park Center.

Then, we will retrace our route, and begin anew from Park headquarters for the route in the opposite direction, clockwise. You will have the Park map, but if you are planning your trip ahead, here is the online map: Recovery of Hawaiʻi Volcanoes National Park - Hawaiʻi Volcanoes National Park (U.S. National Park Service) (nps.gov)

Hawai'i Volcanoes National Park
Visitor Center

Getting there: from Hilo, it's 30 miles south on Highway 11 (a 45-minute drive). From Kailua-Kona, it's a 96 mile drive southeast on Highway 11 (2 to 2 1/2 hour drive). You can't miss the Park entrance. It's particularly fun to drive from Kona. You will drive through the scenic Ka'u desert, and as you approach the Park, you will see signs that say such things as "Watch for cracks on the road."

Make the Visitor Center your first stop! Here you can get free maps and **updates on volcanic activity, and which areas are open, which is information is essential! Park conditions change daily! Even hourly!**
I repeat: Volcanic activity changes constantly, so it is essential to stop at the Visitor Center, and find out what is happening.
Here you can watch fantastic movies of eruptions. **I highly recommend the exciting movie of the 1959 Kilauea Iki eruption**, which is usually shown only once a day. It's fabulous, and in color. You get a real feel for Kilauea Volcano from it. Call ahead to ask what time it is shown: 985-6000. It's free, of course.

There are wonderful and informative displays of Kilauea flora and fauna, featuring the recorded sounds of our rare birds. You can also talk story with the very friendly Park rangers. There are free guided hikes and lectures: times and places are posted by nine-thirty each morning on the board just outside the Center. These are all worthwhile.

You can also obtain backcountry camping permits (free) from the rangers; though not many rangers are out in the backcountry, it is wise to let them know where you are, just in the case of an eruption. It has happened that they

41

have had to evacuate campers and hikers in life-threatening situations, such as unannounced lava flows.

Be sure to fill your water bottles with Kilauea's delicious, filtered rainwater; the tap is just outside the Center by the restrooms. It's the best water on the island!

The Hawaii Pacific Parks Association Bookstore is also located within the Visitor Center. You might want to pick up an inexpensive rain parka here. They also sell nifty sweatshirts and tees with Park logos on them. Just so you can let everyone know you have been to the most active volcano on Earth!.

Volcano House Hotel

Right across the street from the Visitor Center is the Volcano House. Originally a one-room grass shelter built in 1846, made of grass and 'ohi'a wood, the Volcano House is Hawaii's oldest hotel. Mark Twain, in *Roughing It*, was happy to stay there in 1866. He wrote, "Neat, roomy, well furnished and a well kept hotel. The surprise of finding a good hotel at such an outlandish spot startled me, considerably more than the volcano did." It had four bedrooms by then! It's original location however, was across the street, where the Volcano Art Gallery is now.

It's perched right on the rim of Kilauea caldera, and I mean right on the rim! and offers 33 historic rooms. There are beautiful guest rentals throughout the Volcano area, but the views from Volcano House can't be beat!

From the Rim Restaurant and Uncle's George's Lounge, you can normally partake of a fabulous view of the caldera while enjoying good food. Uncle George's Lounge offers take out, and guests may also avail of all-day dining in-room. Food is good! You can see the menu here: https://zmenu.com/volcano-house-dining-room-volcano-2-online-menu/

Uncle George Lycurgus, the "dean of Hawaiian hospitality," purchased the Volcano House in 1904 and managed it until 1921. He sold his interest but got it all back again and managed it until 1960. He died at the ripe old age of 101 in 1960, so he saw a lot of changes at the volcano.

Volcano House now offers 33 rooms, and features stunning views of the Halema'uma'u Crater. Volcano House also takes reservations for the campgrounds at Namakanipaio. There is a section below on beautiful Namakanipaio, the Place of the Conflicting Winds, with its fragrant eucalyptus trees. Both cabins and tents, which the hotel sets up and takes down, are available. The number to reserve a spot is: (844)-569-8849). It's first-come first-serve with no reservations. You can see here for more info: https://www.nps.gov/havo/planyourvisit/namakanipaio-campground.htm

At Volcano House, even if you are not staying as a guest, you can relax in the beautiful reception room, and admire the art and warm up at the usually roaring fireplace.

One great thing do do is get a glass of wine or beer and sit in one of the comfy lounge chairs in front of Uncle George's lounge at sunset. It's an amazing sight to watch darkness creep over the caldera. A truly unforgettable sight.

There are several retail shops within the hotel, which offer the work of local artisans.

Also, enjoy savings of up to 10% if you are a member of the Military, AARP, AAA or if you are kamaaina, a Hawaiian resident.

Call the Volcano House at 808-756-9625.
Email: frontdesk@hawaiivolcanohouse.com
Website: https://www.hawaiivolcanohouse.com/

Volcano Art Gallery

If you're art-inclined, the Volcano Art Gallery, one of if not the most prestigious and selective galleries in Hawaii, is just a few steps west from the Visitor's Center. This was the original 1877 Volcano House, and you can have fun reading the roster of comments in the guest books by visitors, including notables such as Mark Twain.

The Volcano Art Center began in 1971 when Boone Morrison and Franco Salmoiraghi leased the empty 1877 Volcano House, which was now on the National Register of Historic Places as Hawaii's oldest visitor accommodation, for wilderness photography workshops. In 1974, permission to use it on a permanent basis was granted.

Originally just a thatched inn, built in 1866, it had been owned by three men who made their fortune in pulu, the soft golden fiber from the center of the hapu'u fern, which had been used for stuffing furniture. By 1877, visitors from all over the world were watching the lava from Kilauea Caldera from the front porch. The three partners, with the idea of promoting tourism, hired William Lentz to build a larger Volcano House Hotel. Materials were transported from Keauhou coast by horseback and carts, and the rafters, studs and posts were hewn by hand from 'ohi'a and naio trees, just as you see them now.

By 1891, a second level with fourteen rooms was added. In 1921 the Inter-Island Steam Navigation Company took over and built another two-story wing, so that it now had 115 rooms! The 1877 structure was sawed away and moved to its present location. In 1940 Volcano House was destroyed by fire, leaving the 1877 building to serve as lobby, bar and post office, and the new Volcano House Hotel was built at the caldera's edge. The old building was relegated to employee living quarters and furniture storage and fell into disrepair. It was then saved by Morrison and Salmoiraghi in 1971.

The Gallery features several hundred great artists whose work is inspired by Kilauea, and you will find some of the best art in Hawaii here, as the Volcano Art Gallery is very selective. Have a look at the wonderful pit-fired "aumakua" (divine guardian) "mana artifacts" which are usually displayed right on top of the jewelry cases. These are unique, small and make great gifts. If you are looking for woodwork, especially koa, this is the place! If you hit it just right, you might want to attend one of the opening shows. You can ask the great people at the Gallery when the next event is. There is always a special show featuring the best of Hawaii artists.

The Gallery also sponsors workshops, classes, special lectures and hula performances. Their website is http://www.volcanoartcenter.org/ The Gallery is open every day from nine to five, except Christmas day.

Check out the unique pit-fired aumakua sculptures on the counter. They are perfect mementos or gifts to take back home. Created by local artist Uldra Johnson! That's me! My book *Bones of Love: Stories of Old Hawaii* is available there too. If you love Hawaii, you might want to get a copy. Highly recommended!

General Information on the Crater Rim Trail

Much of Crater Rim Trail, the trail which circles Kilauea's summit caldera, was closed, as I wrote before, due to extensive damage from the 2018 eruption, but now you can traverse again much of the very edge of the impressive caldera. You will be walking right along the edge of the immense caldera. *Don't go TOO close!* If you have young children, keep them near you.

You can access the trail from various points, and walk various distances.

It's an easy hike from Volcano House or Volcano Arts Center to Kilauea Overlook and then to Uēkahuna Bluff along Crater Rim Trail, but still take some water. It might be hot and dry, or windy, wet and cold. Stay on the trail! There are cliffs, cracks and steam vents along the way. You will pass through a beautiful koa grove.

For the more interesting hike, follow the path from the Volcano Art Center, through Sulphur Banks, then cross the road at Steaming Bluff (Steam Vents) as described below.

Of course, you can drive too, stopping at the various sites described below.

Let's go!

Halema'uma'u Trail

This trail begins behind the Volcano House. It's a moderate hiking trail and you can choose to hike 0.8 miles one-way to the floor of Kilauea caldera, or you can hike 1.3 miles one-way to the top of Uealoha, Byron Ledge, if it is open. Byron Ledge divides Kilauea caldera from the smaller Kilauea Iki crater. There are some great views into Kilauea caldera from Byron Ledge. From there you can even hike across Kilauea Iki to Nahuku, Thurston Lava Tube. Consult the Park map for various routes from the trail head. Due to the current eruption, the trail may be closed at the point of the caldera floor. **At the time of the current 2021 eruption, the caldera floor is closed, so you will have to retrace your path up.**

This is the trail used by Park visitors since 1846!

From the trail-head, the trail drops 425 feet to the caldera floor. It's a beautiful trail through rainforest made up predominately of the ubiquitous 'Ohi'a trees, hapu'u, the largest tree ferns in the world, 'ama'u ferns, and the lovely and fragrant but invasive Himalayan ginger, which blooms in late July through September. If you visit at this time, there will be a fragrance like you are in heaven! Invasive, yes, but still a flower that looks like it came from another world!

The tree ferns live as long as 1000 years! Believed to be a *kino lau*, a form of the earth goddess Haumea, they reach upward until their weight, mostly water, causes them to topple over. But they don't stop growing! They start growing upward again, and their trunks on the ground become "nurse logs" for many other plants—mosses, ferns, tree seedlings. We here in Volcano treasure our hapu'u!

The 'ama'u ferns are similar to hapu'u, and only the experienced can tell them apart. They are smaller than hapu'u, and their fronds branch only once, while hapu'u fronds branch twice. Can you tell them apart? They are considered a kino lau of the demi-god pig-man Kamapua'a, the would-be lover of Pele. But in the big fight between them (she finds him repulsive), ultimately she wins, and he transforms into the 'ama'u fern to escape her fury.

Ah the lovely 'ohi'a trees! They flower year round, but are most profuse in summer. You don't have to watch too closely to see that their blossoms, lehua, are nectar to the red 'apapane bird and the yellow 'amakihi bird. The birds and the 'ohi'a trees existence are intimately intertwined. If you see a yellow or even more rarely, a white one, know that you have seen something special indeed.

I love the area with the big boulders! I always feel like hugging them! These fell from the crater rim during the 1983 6.6 magnitude earthquake. You'll see a lot of reddish fibrous structures hanging from 'ohi'a trees in this area—these are believed to be caused by stress. The earth quake stressed the 'ohi'a trees and caused these aerial roots to grow.

Just off the trail you might see a big boulder with words carved into it: *B Boyd, J Webster, Yacht Wanderer, and 51*. Kilroy was here! Boyd and Webster, an adventurer and an artist, who sailed together on the boat, Yacht Wanderer, visited here in 1851. Boyd was later killed by natives in Guadalcanal, but Webster survived a later sinking of the yacht, made his way to New Zealand, and wrote a book about his adventures: *The Last Cruise of the Wanderer*.

Notice how as you get to the bottom near the caldera the terrain changes. You can stand at the bottom of the trail on the caldera floor, but most probably, traversing the caldera floor at this time is forbidden. But you can look out upon the frozen lava floor, imagining what it looked like when it was a huge lake of molten lava. See how quickly it is being repopulated with 'ohi'a and ferns. One day, barring an overflow of lava, it again will be dense forest. On the other hand, it may again be a lake of fire.

You can read more about this beautiful trail in the Park free guide: Halemaʻumaʻu Trail Guide (nps.gov).

But, all things that go up must come down, and all things that come down, must go up. Retrace the path, if the caldera floor is closed and take your time, and enjoy this rainforest wonderland.

Sulphur Banks
Ha'akulamanu

You can walk to the Sulphur Banks by taking the trail just a few minutes from the Volcano Art Gallery, or, you can drive a half-mile and park at the Steam Vents and walk back a short distance, cross the road and access the walking trail. It's simple to find. If you choose to walk, which I suggest, from the Visitor's Center, turn west, the opposite direction from the Park entrance. Take the sidewalk trail past the Volcano Art Center. Follow it until it forks, and take the right fork as it descends downward.

Do you know what sulphur smells like? Rotten eggs! This area is filled with *fumarole*s, which are holes in volcanic areas from which hot smoke and gases escape. **If you have heart or respiratory problems, or if you are pregnant or have children, you should avoid this area.**

Sulphur dioxide and hydrogen sulfide react to produce pure sulphur, that beautiful yellow mineral you see, which was called kukaepele, the poop of Pele, by the ancient Hawaiians. You can also see gypsum, hematite, and opal, the whitish milky glaze.

This fascinating place, which might remind you of Yellowstone, was anciently called Ha'akulamanu, which means "like a birds' gathering place." It was famous for both its birds and its vapors. The gases inhibited the growth of deep-rooted trees, creating habitat for foraging birds, including Nene, the endangered state bird, and other geese and ducks.

The lovely boarded walk is bounded by 'ohi'a lehua trees, wild bamboo orchids, and many types of ferns, including the abundant false stag horn fern. There are several benches where you can rest, have a snack, take pics and enjoy the views.

There is a lovely view of Mauna Loa at the top of the boardwalk, if it isn't clouded over. I like to come here in the afternoon, when it is usually sunny, bask in the sunshine while sitting on the bench, and absorb the majesty of the biggest mountain on Earth. At this time of day, Mauna Loa takes on lovely subdued hues of deep purples, blues and grays, which contrast beautifully with the golds, silvers, pinks, and ivory shades of the sedge grasses. Wintertime is especially beautiful here; the low lighting of the sun makes this a stunning place to photograph.

It's also lovely on misty days, with the steam rising all around. In fact, it's always lovely! But on a misty day, the colors are saturated, and you can get beautiful photos.

My fave time of year however, is fall, because the fountain grasses turn lovely shades of silver, gold, copper and pink. And the sunlight is low, so that there is a mysterious glow all around.

Surface water leaking into cracks where it is heated to high temperatures rises as steam and toxic gasses here, turning the earth a reddish color, and coating the rocks with the beautiful crystals, such as the yellow sulphur crystals. Please don't hop off the boardwalk to gather crystals; not only is it unlawful and disrespectful, but you can be severely burned if your foot goes through the sometimes shallow earth. It has happened! *Keep your children on the trail, for their safety.*

You can retrace your steps, or cross the road and walk over to Steam Vents.

Steam Vents
Wahinekapu

Steam Vents is a five-minute drive from the Park Visitor Center, or you can walk the trail past the Volcano Art Center, as just described above and through Sulphur Banks. Although steam vents occur throughout the Park, this is a great place to stop and see them up close. These are fumaroles of steam but no gasses, so you can get very near and even feel the heat. Just to one side, clearly marked, is access to the Crater Rim Trail, which runs approximately 10.6 miles around the entire Kilauea Caldera, though portions (almost half) are now closed due to the road damage caused by the last eruption, as previously explained.

If you drive, you can walk across the street to the Sulphur Banks trail.

If you want to, from here you can walk all the way (1.8 miles one way) to the Kilauea overlook and then to Uēkahuna Bluff, just before the site of the Jaggar Museum and old Volcano Observatory and back, rather than drive. I recommend it. It's lovely especially on a full moon evening. Take a flash light though. And a rain parka. Or, perhaps you might just want to stroll the trail a short distance and peer over the cliff. **Don't get too close to the edge! It crumbles easily and there might be an overhang.** A man recently did just this and died there, so be careful.

The steam vents here exude more steam just after a heavy rain; that's because the water seeps down, down, down to the hot cracks, is heated, and rises up again as vapor. These vents, unlike the one ones across the street at Sulphur Banks, which are much deeper, are not toxic but they are hot!

I wish I could find out why the Hawaiians called this place Wahinekapu. Wahine means girl, woman and kapu means taboo. But so far I haven't found out why!

Kilauea Military Camp (KMC)

KMC is one- mile west past the Visitor Center and Steam Vents. You will see a grassy lawn and neat row of cottages. In the center of the cottages is the Front Desk building, which is always open. KMC sits on 52 acres of its own within the Park's 300,000 acres. It was established the same year as the Park, 1916. Originally a military training facility, it has served as a Navy camp, an internment camp, a prisoner-of-war camp, and now a recreational camp for the military.

KMC is open to all active duty and retired Armed Forces (Army, Navy, Marine Corps, Air Force and Coast Guard), Reserve, National Guard, and Other Uniformed Services (Public Health Service, National Oceanic and Atmospheric Administration.) Also, Armed Forces dependents, current and retired Department of Defense (DOD) civilian employees including Coast Guard Civilian Employees, and sponsored guests. (Other personnel on official business with the Department of Defense may also be eligible.)

From their current web page: Valid military ID or Department of Defense ID required for check-in.

Reservations accepted up to a year in advance

Prices are subject to change without notice.

Pets, firearms, and fireworks are prohibited.

A one night deposit by Check, Money Order, Visa, MasterCard or American Express is required within 15 of your booking date.

For reservations:
808-967-8333 or 808-967-8335

usarmy.kmc-reservations@mail.mil

If you are military personnel or retired military, you may shop at the little general store, They *do* ask for military documentation, *most* of the time, if you know what I mean. It is currently open every day, from 8 a.m. to 7 p. m. Monday – Saturday and 8 to 4 on Sundays. They have food, drinks, toiletries, firewood and a fair selection of Hawaiiana gifts.

There's a post office and bowling alley as well at KMC. There's also a fitness center, with a sauna! There's a tennis and basketball court and a game room. If it's after five, you may get gas there too, at the self-serve pumps, even if you are not military. One day a week there is a great discount at the gas pump, but which day it will be is always a surprise (go figure!) There are also two laundry facilities.

KMC boasts three eating establishments. The Crater Rim is a casual restaurant featuring in the main island cuisine. It offers special holiday menus at Christmas, Thanksgiving, Easter, etc. It currently has modified hours. Lots of locals eat there as well as visitors.

The 10-Pin Grill is located in the bowling alley, and offers burgers, pizza, dinner specials, and also beer and wine. It's usually open Monday through Friday but currently has modified hours.

The Java Cafe is normally open every day, and features Starbucks coffee, muffins, yogurt, smoothies, island coffee, etc. Unfortunately, at present it is closed.

The Lava Lounge, open every evening, features live music on the week-ends. Call 808) 967-8365 after 4 pm for info.

Anyone can eat in the eateries at KMC, no military card needed.

There is a shuttle service from Hilo Airport for $20.00 one way. You must make your reservation for the shuttle at least 48 hours in advance. It departs KMC three times a day, and picks up from Hilo three times a day:

Airport pick-up (Mon-Fri): 11am, 1:30pm, & 3:45pm

Airport drop-off (Mon-Fri): 8:30am, 12 noon, & 2:30pm

No refund for charges or cancellations within 72 hours of the reserved shuttle/tour time. Allow 1 hour travel time each way from Hilo. 20% discount with Military ID's.
After Hours Phone Number: (808) 967-8335, or
(808) 967-8335

KMC is a great place to stay, a lot of bang for the buck. It's super clean, quiet and of course, convenient to the Park!
At Christmas time, KMC decorates all the cottages that line the road. It's a treat to see the old-fashioned lights and embellishments.
Ask at the desk for directions to the gas pump. It is open all day and night but takes credit or debit cards only.
The KMC website is here: http://kilaueamilitarycamp.com/

Kilauea Overlook

Continuing 0.7 miles along Crater Rim Drive by car, past KMC, or hiking Crater Rim Trail toward Jaggar Museum from Steam Vents, as just described above, you reach Kilauea Overlook and then Uēkahuna Bluff, two of the best views of the caldera,

You may see colorful, sacred offerings of stones wrapped in ti leaves and leis of flowers left here on the ground or hung about in trees. Uēkahuna Bluff is sacred ancient ground—please be very respectful. Be careful, as I said above, not to step too close to the edge; many places along the cliff are undercut and the rock is fragile and easily shatters—it's a long way down!

There is parking and there are covered picnic tables at Kilauea Overlook just to the side of the trail, but at lunchtime, these are usually taken by the bicycle tourists. Plan lunch earlier than eleven or later than one o'clock if you want to use the tables. Otherwise, if it is not wet, spread a blanket on the ground and enjoy!

Kilauea Overlook is especially beautiful at night and at dawn. If you can, plan to come in the dark. And better yet, come on a full moon. This is a great place to meditate on eternity, on birth, on death. What better place to contemplate such things than at the edge of the most active volcano on Earth?

This is perhaps the best overlook of Halema'uma'u, the *House of Everlasting Fire*, the home of the fire goddess herself, who is also the goddess of death and rebirth, as far as experiencing the sheer majesty of Kilauea with a minimum of noise and chaos, and pushing and shoving for photos. There are hoards of tourists at Uēkahuna, especially in the early evening, but of course, you should go there too.

One of Pele's names is Ka Wahine 'ai Honua, *the woman who devours the land*. She's often depicted as a wanderer, and people claim to have sighted her all over the Islands, but especially around here, in Kilauea. If you meet a beautiful woman here, or an old beggar woman with a white dog asking for food or drink, be nice to her! Those who are unkind to her are punished by having their lands consumed by lava!

At night I sometimes sit on the big rocks near the edge of the cliff overhang (but not *too* close), kept silent company by only a few skeletal, grey 'ohi'a trees that stand like strange, many-armed sentinels in the moonshine. On a cold and clear night (and if it is clear here at the Volcano, it will most likely be cold—bring a good jacket!), the stars of the Milky Way spread out across the inky-blue sky like a celestial mantle, and the moon hangs high in the sky like a gleaming skull. The three-mile-wide crater looks like a moonscape; huge black boulders are strewn across the otherwise barren and silvery landscape, casting bloated, malformed shadows across the caldera floor. Transparent, whitish steam rises like mute, wispy specters from scattered vents on the floor of the crater, curling and trailing and disappearing into thin air, and the congealed iridescent black lava lake contrasts eerily with the white-striated walls of the caldera. Awed into complete silence by the otherworldly spectacle before me, sometimes the hair on my arms stands up.

Hundreds of feet below, the pit crater, Halema'uma'u, the House of Everlasting Fire, the home of Goddess Pele, is sometimes a lava lake, glowing an intense fiery red-orange. Also sometimes, like a huge, silent ghost, a thick white plume rolls from out of the pit, billowing into the sky high above the caldera, spiraling off toward the sea and the stars, unceasingly.

Awesome!

Uēkahuna Bluff
(May be closed if the Nene are nesting nearby)

Uēkahuna Bluff, at an elevation of 4000 feet, the site of Jaggar Museum and the old Volcano Observatory, means "Wailing Priest." This is where ancient and modern priests made and make their offerings to goddess Pele, who presides over *Ke Lua o Pele*, the pit of Pele. At night, you have a view of the fiery pit; during the day, you can see for miles around in every direction.

It is said that once here on or near this cliff, a house stood over a pit; if anyone entered, the presiding *kahuna* (priest) pulled ropes which made the floor collapse and cause the person to fall to his death. Later, a hero by the name of Kamiki torched the house and the priest wept. That is why the bluff here is called Uēkahuna. "Uwe" means to wail, and "kahuna" means priest.

Sometimes, sitting out here alone on cold, clear full moon nights, I have almost heard the priest keening in the wind.

Aia la o Pele. There is Pele.

There are maybe as many as seven pit craters in the caldera floor below, each inside the other. Just below the surface, at times, a molten lava lake, pure magma, is sloshing and churning and boiling. The red glow that can be seen then is the reflection of the lake. That plume is made up of incredibly toxic gases. We could have a full-on eruption at any time.

Though the scene below, the moonlight and starlight illuminating the ghostly white plume issuing out of the red glow may be eerily soundless, you may sense a vibration just below the threshold of sound, a feeling just below the brink of hearing, coming up through the souls of your feet. It's the movement and flowing of the molten lava below. That's why we have the earthquakes almost everyday; the earth is moving and shifting continuously. Most people aren't sensitive enough to feel it. But I feel it when I lie in bed at night, here in the Village.

At the closed Jaggar Museum, located next door to the closed Hawaiian Volcano Observatory, which is closed to the public, you can get an up-close view of Halema'uma'u—in the past you could watch the seismographs at the now defunct observatory, which were fascinating. Those days are gone for now—the buildings are too precarious perched on the cliff.

If you learn all about volcanoes, you will learn all about the different types of lava *ejecta*—my faves are the ones called Pele's tears and Pele's hair. Pele's hair is made of volcanic glass threads formed when particles of molten material are thrown into the air and spun out by the wind into long, hair-like strands. The diameter of the strands is less than 0.5 mm, and they can be as long as 2 meters and are a deep yellow or gold. Pele's tears are small pieces of solidified lava drops formed when airborne particles of molten material fuse into tear-like drops of volcanic glass. They are jet black in color and are often found on one end of a strand of Pele's hair. You might see some as you walk about.

That great hole below you was a molten lake until 1924. During Captain Cooks' time, Halema'uma'u Crater was 800 ft deep and a lava lake was formed. It was only 1500 feet across. In 1924, Halema'uma'u Crater erupted explosively. Hot magma at a temperature of 2100 degrees Fahrenheit reached the base of the crater. Throughout the eruption, hot molten lava filled up the crater and formed a lava lake. The lava lake then drained to the east of Kilauea. Huge blocks of the crater wall were melted and torn off by the lava flows. The drainage of the lava lake caused the base of the crater to thin and groundwater broke through the crust, reaching the hot lava and causing a series of huge steam explosions. Water and lava don't mix too well!

The eruption in 1924 caused Halema'uma'u to increase in size to 3000 ft wide and 1200 ft deep. Numerous eruptive episodes since then have filled the crater to its present form. The last major eruption occurred in 1967. Lava from the 1967 eruption once filled up the crater to100 ft below its rim. Lava then drained back into the magma chamber.

On May 17, 2018, Kilauea erupted at the summit shooting ash 30,000 feet into the sky. Continued explosive activity at the summit caused a months-long closure of sections of Hawai'i Volcanoes National Park. Lava flows in lower Puna, the eastern side of the island, sent rivers of molten rock into the ocean destroying all of Hawaii's largest natural freshwater lake, and covering substantial portions of residential areas. Lava also filled Kapoho Bay and extended new land nearly a mile into the sea. Seven hundred and sixteen dwellings were destroyed by lava. By early August the eruption subsided substantially, and the last active lava was reported at the surface on September 4. On December 5, 2018, after 90 days of inactivity from the volcano, the eruption that began in 1983 was declared to have ended.

On December 20, 2020, an eruption broke out in, Halema'uma'u, with the lava boiling off a water lake that had been growing for more than a year and replacing it with a lava lake. The lava lake reached a depth of 180 590 feet by late December, but eruptive activity steadily decreased in 2021, with the lava depth increasing to 738 feet by April 2021. On May 26, 2021, Kilauea was no longer erupting. Lava supply to the lava lake appeared to have ceased between May 11 and May 13, and the lava lake had completely crusted over by May 20. The last surface activity in Halema'uma'u was observed on May 23, 2021.

At the end of this guide, I describe the 2018 eruption in more detail. Interesting time!

The view here, under any conditions, is fab. Not only can you peer into the yawning mouth of Halema'uma'u, but you can look for miles off into the Ka'u desert. Ask a ranger to point out Mauna Ulu if it is clear. Mauna Ulu is a place you probably will want to visit later.

Formerly, the Crater Rim Drive offered world-class cycling; I often used to cycle around the thirteen mile (10. 6 miles officially) scenic route in awe, and hopefully some day will be able to do it again.

You may see beautiful white birds soaring gracefully above the crater. These are koa'e, white-tailed tropic birds. They feed in the sea, but they nest here in the crater walls. They plunge dive 50 to 65 feet into the ocean to catch their prey of fish and squid. They are related to boobies and frigate birds. They breed in colonies and pairs mate for life. At the beginning of the breeding season, they engage in complex aerial gymnastics. Nests are placed in hard-to-reach locations on cliffs as well as in caves and tree hollows; nests have little if any material. In Hawaii, breeding occurs March through October and a single egg is laid per season. Both parents incubate the egg, and brood and feed the chick.

If you come during day-light hours, look toward the south—you can spot the **Southwest Rift**, a great series of cracks running from Kilauea's summit all the way to the sea. That means you are standing upon a major earthquake fault!

The Southwest Rift Zone of Kilauea is almost entirely located within Hawai'i Volcanoes National Park and has its own unique volcanic land-forms, such as the Great Crack, the Kamakai'a Hills, and Pu'ukoa'e Unlike the heavily forested East Rift Zone, much of the Southwest Rift Zone lies downwind of Halema'uma'u in the Ka'u Desert, with its sparse vegetation near the summit and scattered grasslands closer to the coast. Due to a lack of roads and only a few hiking trails. It is infrequently visited.

Looking toward the direction of the Southwest Rift, you will see windswept, sandy, boulder-strewn explosive deposits blanketing older lava flows, deposits of explosive eruptions that began around 1500 and continued until the early 19th century. One of the most famous of these eruption occurred in 1790, and resulted in the deaths of several hundred people traveling through the region, some of whose footprints are said to be preserved in the ash deposits. More about that later. It's a place you can visit and I highly recommend!

See those three dark, symmetrical volcanic cones? Those are the Kamakai'ia Hills. Their Hawaiian name means "the eye of the fish," because the cones, each dimpled with a cup-shaped crater, reminded early Hawaiians of the eyes of fish such as ulua. The cones are the largest of a series of vents, including older, more eroded cones, spatter ramparts, and large ground cracks, that spewed lava lumps and blocks of older rock in the past. Multiple eruptions have originated along this three-mile long mini-rift over a period spanning at least 500 years. During explosive eruptive phases, volcanic bombs, rubble-like scoria, and spatter were spewed. Some of the largest bombs are more than three feet in diameter! Another interesting thing is that the lava in the Kamakai'a Hills is like no other on Kilauea.

Look to the southwest from the Kamakai'a Hills and you will see three more hills, the cones of Pu'ukoa'a, formed during an eruption more than 200 years ago.

Recent eruptions in the Southwest Rift zone occurred in 1868, 1919–1920, 1971, and 1974. Some relatively small eruptions that lasted a few days or less, such as the eruption of 1868. One lasted eight months, the more voluminous eruption of Mauna Iki in 1919–1920. The last Southwest Rift Zone eruption was the short-lived December 1974 event in which lava flowed more than seven miles from a series of fissure vents that opened a few miles south of Halema'uma'u.

Reminder: If you come at night, perhaps during a full moon, bring something warm and water proof! The wind can be quite cold!

You might imagine that, many years ago, one solitary kahuna lived on this very spot, the guardian of the great fire goddess Pele, offering sacrifices continuously for her happiness. You might imagine his lonely life, measured by the cycles of the moon, compensated for his isolation by the sheer majesty and mystery of existence.

****

Around Crater Rim
Clockwise

Retracing the route back to the Park Center, take your time if you are driving, don't let tailgaters push you, and enjoy the changes of scenery. You're in Hawaii!

If you are hiking, also take your time, and remember not to go too close to the edge. It has happened! (Haven't I said this before?)

The next portion of this guide begins at the Park Center, traveling in a clockwise direction. So drive back toward the visitor center.

From the Park Visitor Center, turn left toward the gate and take a right on Crater Rim Drive East, which will take you to all its wonderful sights and on to the breathtaking Chain of Craters Road.

First stop—Kilauea Iki, "Little Kilauea."

Kilauea Iki Overlook
and
Kilauea Iki Trail

From the visitor center, turn left and then right onto Crater Rim Drive. If you are coming through the entrance gate, Crater Rim Drive, look sharp, it will be the first street on your left. The Kilauea Iki overlook is about a twisting mile from the stop sign on Crater Rim Road. Hang a left at the stop sign and leisurely enjoy the forest drive.

Kilauea Iki is not to be missed! This is the most popular hike in the park. And a world class hike! I've trekked it more than 3000 times! Almost every day for years! It's always new! Even if you just park at Kilauea Iki overlook and peer down into the crater, this is a scene you will always remember. Just about 60 years ago, in 1959, the highest and hottest lava fountain ever recorded in Hawaiian history, 1900 feet! spewed spectacular fireworks like never seen before, creating a wide, flat lake of black lava 414 feet deep. Looking down from the top at almost 500 feet onto the congealed lava, which appears as a sea of black waves, people appear as ants traversing the caldera floor, still steaming through cracks and rifts in the crust. Notice the hill of red cinder cone. That's Pu'u Pua'i.

On November 14, 1959, a lava wall burst from a fissure directly across from where you are standing. During the next five weeks, 17 separate lava "episodes" occurred, causing molten lava to flow in and out of the original 800 feet crater. The red cinder cone was created at this time, Pu'u Pua'i, and it is the hole at the bottom of the cone, not visible here, but visible if you hike below, from which the lava poured fourth. When it stopped, this is what was left, a slowly cooling lava lake, which had filled up one half of the original crater.

If you can, hike this one! This is a world class hike! This is a must do!

From the Kilauea Iki parking lot, as you are overlooking the crater, take the trail to your left. You can also take the trail to your right, but I will describing the trail to the left, clock-wise.

This a one-mile trek down into the crater, a mile across the crater, and then about two mile back up and around the other side—doable by most people in 2-4 hours, depending on how long you stop to smell the roses! I often see little children happily trekking along, as well as tiny babies on their mother or father's back. (I also often see tired little children happily being carried on someone's back.) Fairly elderly people in good condition also can do this hike, though, remember, there is a 400 feet plus climb back out of the caldera, the equivalent of a 40 high story building!

If you want to take a shorter hike, descend down to the bottom of the crater, take a good look, and come back up the same way. That will make a two-mile hike.

You must take water, and I recommend light rain gear. Weather conditions can change in a moment. Wearing layers is best, because it can be chilly or very hot, all in one hike! You might also take sunscreen.

Begin by taking a long look from the overlook at the incredible landscape below you. Iki last erupted in August 1959. Once twice as deep at 800 feet, lava from the surprise eruption filled the crater to approximately 400 feet as you see it now. That red cinder cone you see to your right, Pu'u Pua'i, was formed. Downwind from the cinder cone, the forests were completely denuded. Fountains reaching as high as 180 meters enthralled thousands of visitors who were allowed to watch it from where you are standing now! That wouldn't be allowed today! Ha! Times have changed! Eventually, the fountaining was 580 meters (1,900 feet) high! That's five times the height of that red cinder cone!

The floor you see now was a molten lava lake, seething and frothing with its waves breaking against the sides of the crater like waves at the beach. Suddenly, the fountaining stopped as quickly as it started, going from 210 meters high to just a few gas bubbles in less than a minute. The 1959 episode was over.

Lava tubes directly connected to Iki are responsible for the 'Aila'au eruption of the 15th century, which erupted for 60 years, covering much of the Puna district. Lava from a vent near the eastern end of Iki erupted and covered 166 square miles. In comparison the 2018 lava flow covered less than one-tenth that area. The eruption occurred before written records, but the ancient Hawaiians recorded it in oral traditions and it is the basis for the name, 'Aila'au, which means "forest eater." Thurston Lava Tube, Nahuku, which we will soon visit, was created during the 'Aila'au erupting.

Lucky you! You are about to embark on one of the most unique treks on the planet, a descent through a lush rainforest filled with rare birds and exotic plants into the bleak moon-like landscape of an active volcano!

The path begins in the high rainforest. At Kilauea Iki overlook, facing the caldera, head up the path to your left. As you traverse the lush tropical jungle, you will meet the King (the koa tree) and Queen (the 'ohi'a lehua tree) of the forest and their minions, the native plants and animals of the islands, of which more than 90% are endemic, found nowhere else on planet Earth. There are several scenic viewpoints along the first part of the half-mile distance to the lava tube; stop and take them in. Careful!

Notice the deep cracks on your left on the trail. These are the kinds of cracks you can fall into if you go off trail!

In a half-mile, the trail comes to the Thurston Lava Tube parking lot. You can cross the road and explore it now, in which case, see the next section below. Or, stay on the sidewalk on the same side of the road, and the trail picks up again in just a few yards on your right and descends. You can then explore lava tube later.

Descend into the crater via a lovely rainforest switchback one-mile trail, easy-going. Enjoy the birds! Stop at the bottom when you come out of the forest and just spend some time taking in the surreal scene before you! Notice the jagged ring of rocks surrounding the entire crater—this is called the bathtub ring, because the successive 17 episodes of lava flows ran back into Puu Pua'i, leaving this ring of rock behind, just like the dirty ring around a bathtub. It is of interest that the NASA Mars rover was tested in this crater. Not hard to see why. Where is MJ?

Now you will then experience the surreal, thrilling one-mile walk across what once was a molten lava lake, now hardened rope-like *pahoehoe* lava and sharp, treacherous *a'a* lava, surrounded by almost 500 foot cliffs. Where else in the world can you walk on lava in the caldera of a volcano active only 50 years ago?

Hawks, kolea birds and clouds soar high overhead, and to your left in the distance is Pu'u Pua'i (Gushing Hill) cinder cone, that red cinder cone you saw earlier from the top of the path.

Notice the stacks of rocks. These are *ahu*; originally the native Hawaiians used them to mark boundaries. Here a few mark the trail. But all these at the beginning of the trail are a sort of statement by some tourists—as in— *Kilroy was here*! Some are quite precariously balanced. The Park discourages such artistic statements as being culturally inappropriate and occasionally the Rangers come around and knock them down.

You don't have to stay on the trail here, which is clearly discernible, but do **remember the Hawaiian adage regarding walking on lava—*keep your mouth shut and your eyes to the ground.*** Take your time and stroll over to some of the steam vents if you wish. This steam results from rainwater vaporizing on the hot rock below the surface. Be careful—it's hot!

You might notice some pipes sticking out of the ground on your right on the trail. These are drill holes used to measure the lava lake's temperature and rate of solidification. The first drilling took place four months after the eruption, but stopped at nine feet because molten lava was hit. The last time drilling was done, in 1988, only small traces of molten lava, *melt*, remained at depths of 240-330 feet.

Just some interesting facts from the Park's scientists: The lava lake weighs 235 times more than the Empire State Building. Approximately 86 *million* tons of lava poured into the crater from the source during the 1959 eruption. The lake is solid but still cooling; the floor continues to subside approximately three quarters of an inch annually as it cools.

As you head across the crater, you might wonder about the white lines, which remind me of the Nazca geo-glyphs in Peru; they are deposits of calcium sulfates and silica, deposited by the steam. Notice the raised terraces, or islands. They were created when gigantic blocks of Pu'u Pua'i slid into the molten lake and rafted away from the base of the cone.

Pu'u Pua'i, the big red cinder cone about half way across the crater, is the mouth from which all the lava that filled the lake was belched. You can get very close for a good look. There is a little path up over the hillock that is safe to walk as you near it. Just be careful. This is a good place to scout around and look at the titanium lava rocks, the beautiful rainbow-hued shards that change colors in the sunlight. **Don't take any, though**. Strictly forbidden! I will know, because I often stop to admire their magic! Besides, they don't seem to sparkle once removed from their home. Please leave them where you find them.

Notice also the different colors of rock. The bright red is iron. It's almost magical how different minerals are created from the same uniform substance, magma. I've asked a number of scientists about this—the truth is, no one can explain exactly how different substances can come from one substance.

If you look closely, you can see how slabs of spatter have slid down the cone. The cone has changed very much just in the last 10 years—once it was almost perfectly rounded. I remember when.

The sharp and treacherous lava over which you are walking looks like a'a lava, but it actually is made of fused blobs of molten lava which rolled down the cone, breaking up into the clinkery, jagged chunks you see now. The rocks weigh less than you would expect—gas bubbles from the frothy lava left holes which cause them to be light weight, though sharp!

Take your time and enjoy! As you approach the trail ascending up through the rainforest, you might hear the call of the i'o, the Hawaiian hawk that lives on the cliff above. You might even get a glimpse of him.

The caldera may be hot and windy, cold and rainy, misty or foggy—whatever! And conditions may change in a moment! I've never seen snow (ha!) but once I was caught in a majestic though very frightening lightening storm when I was the only person down there. (Duh!) Often, ethereal rainbows appear like magic through the steaming vents on the caldera floor. You can see them on misty days after crossing the first half of the crater. If you happen to be down in Iki on such a day, turn around once in a while and look back toward where you have traversed. I've had the thrill of walking into one.

Truly an alien landscape, Kilauea Iki may make you feel as if you have been on the moon!

Nahuku
Thurston Lava Tube

Less then a half-mile drive continuing from the Kilauea Iki overlook, you will come to the parking lot for Thurston Lava Tube, Nahuku. Often it is filled. So if can, walk there in a few minutes from the Kilauea Iki parking lot.

Nahuku (the Protuberances), known more commonly as Thurston Lava Tube, is one of the most visited sites in the Park. Everyone is fascinated by caves!

Tip! Come in the morning, before nine, or in the evening, after five. Otherwise, due to its popularity, you may not find a parking place, and also, you won't get to visit the cave without a crowd of people. It's one of the most popular sites in the Park. Nahuku Lava Tube, Thurston Lava tube, is one of the few lava tubes that are open to the public. You might want to bring a flashlight, though the cave is lit. Your cell phone light will be fine.

Nahuku Crater is an emerald jewel set within the Hawaiian rainforest, with its delicate lacy ferns hanging like lace curtains over the mouth of the prehistoric and VERY eerie Thurston lava tube.

The trail consists of a short walk down into the crater through dense vegetation as it steeply descends. The trail then goes through a short section of the 600 feet lava tube. This portion is well lit (normally) and has a macadam floor; that is why there are puddles of rainwater that have seeped down through the ceiling of the cave and not downward into the porous lava. Those long, stringy things hanging from the ceiling are roots of 'ohi'a trees.

Note: for those who have trouble walking, start at the opposite end of the tube and retrace your steps. Instead of following the sign to the lava tube, turn toward the restrooms, walk up the gradual incline, and toward all the people coming out of the cave. Then, you can retrace your steps and avoid the steep stairs at the entrance.

It's awesome to reflect that just a few hundred years ago, a river of molten red lava rushed through this lava tube thirty miles to the sea!

What exactly is a lava tube?

A lava tube is a natural conduit formed by flowing lava which drains, forming a channel from a volcano during an eruptive event. The roof and sides form a crust which hardens while the flowing lava begins either to cool, or, pushes its way deeper. As the lava moves further away from the point of eruption, it can begin to flow in unchanneled, fan-like streams. These are pahoehoe flows.

You can think of lava tube formation as rivulets of molten lava that freeze on the outside, forming a channel that allows the interior to remain molten and continue to flow. In effect, they are self-creating channels. A lava tube is very much like a living thing! Like blood veins!

Look for the step marks on the walls of lava tubes which indicate the depths at which the lava flowed; these are flow lines. Flows are not always continuous in a tube; they can stop and begin again—hence the different flow lines.

The tubes can be of different lengths. A tube from the Mauna Loa flow of 1859 flowed 31 miles and into the sea. But that's nothing compared to the lava tubes on planet Venus, which channeled lava hundreds of miles!

Thurston lava tube is an extinct tube, which means the lava flow has ceased and cooled, and left this cave. It was discovered in 1913 by Lorrin Thurston, a local newspaper publisher; hence its name. When it was first discovered, before people pried them off, lava stalactites hung from the ceiling.

Emerging through a natural skylight, the trail loops back to some bathrooms (be prepared—primitive!) and then the starting point.

You used to have the option of continuing through the cave but this option is no longer available, unfortunately, because this is the most interesting section of the lava tube.

In the past, you could climb down into this part of the tube very warily, and if you dared, make your way very, very carefully all the way to the end. You would have to skirt huge boulders and fallen piles of rocks and hop over puddles of rainwater. You could marvel at the frozen black lava "push-ups" on the floor of the cave (remember those ice-cream push-ups? These lava push-ups are named for those!) and the sparkling rainbow titanium "drinking straws" that dangle from the lofty cathedral-like ceiling.

At the end of the cave, you could turn off your flashlights, sit in total darkness, and total silence, on a newly-fallen-from-the-ceiling lava stone "bench," (happened in the summer of 2010! Yikes!) and listen to the haunting sound of water drops seeping through the roof of the cave.

But not any more! That convenient newly-fallen stone bench is now covered with a many-ton portion of the ceiling of the cave! Luckily, it fell at night when no one happened to be sitting there! For now, for safety's sake, this portion of the tube is closed.

If you are really adventurous, you can visit the open part of Nahuku at night. It's permitted by Park regulations. My friends and I sometimes come here, go deep into the cave, and chant the Hallelujah chorus. Awesome!

Pu'upua'i (Gushing Hill) Overlook

Next stop on Crater Rim is Pu'upua'i. Head on from Thurston lava tube down a beautiful winding forest road. Enjoy but watch out for bicyclists.

Pu'upua'i is the giant red cinder cone that formed during the eruption at Kilauea Iki Crater in 1959. It is visible from many areas along Crater Rim and Kilauea Iki trails. **It will be the first stop after passing Thurston Lava tube.** You can park here, or you can go on a very short distance and park at Devastation Trail, then hike the one-half mile to Pu'upua'i. Or, you can park here, and hike over to Devastation Trail. Lots of choices!

The cone formed during the 1959 eruption as lava from the 1,900 foot high fountains cooled in the air and fell down as cinder.

Devastation Trail, you will see the sign, could be called Restoration Trail, as the native plants and animals reclaim what was taken 50 years ago by the Kilauea Iki eruption. I love the shades of colors—the rich browns, golds, tawny fawns, and the bright red of the fire plant (though it is an invasive). It's less than a half-mile walk and you can retrace your steps.

From the viewing platform, you can over look into Kilauea Iki. You might see the soaring tropic birds just below you, and once in a while, the i'o, the hawk.

There is a picnic table here, and this is a great place to lunch. It's quiet and majestic as you look down 400 feet below into Kilauea Iki. Usually not many people are here, so you can get a good hit of the scenery.

If you hike from here over Devastation trail, please remember this is a very delicate reforestation area. Stay on the trail please.

Please see the description just below for more information on the Devastation Trail area.

Devastation Trail and Desolation Peak

Desolation Peak can be accessed from two directions. You can go by way of hiking across Byron's Ledge, from the direction of Kilauea Iki, or you can drive to it.

Don't want to hike? Then drive.

The easy way, of course, to reach Devastation Trail is to drive past Thurston Lava Tube, continuing on about two miles (lots of curves, watch for cyclists; I might be one of them!) past the first road on the right (Pu'u Pua'i Overlook) to the next road on the right. Here you will find a large parking area.

There are two gentle trails—explore both! The paved one-half mile trail leads to Pu'u Pua'i Overlook, which you passed on the way here and which I described just above. This area is wheelchair and stroller accessible. Do take it; the trail itself is interesting and you can totter on the sheer cliff side and look down into Kilauea Iki. It's less than a half-mile easy meandering. There are tree molds along the way and other interesting wonders, such as Pele's tears and hairs. Pele's hair is the term for threads of volcanic glass which form when particles of molten lava are thrown into the air and spun out by the wind into long, hair-like strands. Pele's tears are created when air born particles of lava cool and harden in the shape of...teardrops.

There is also a picnic table here, one of the few in the Park, and it is usually available. A wonderful place to lunch.

The plant life here has all taken root since the 1959 eruption. Nature abhors a vacuum! You can see 'ohi'a and ohelo, being among the first to recolonize a lava environment. There are also non-native invasives you may recognize, like blackberry, Japanese anemone (lovely even if invasive), fireplant (the beautiful bright red ground cover and buddleia.

The other unpaved trail is even more interesting. It's really just a short walk to Desolation Peak.

This area was once a large 'ohi'a forest, but when Kilauea Iki blew up in 1959, the trees were denuded; the white bleached bones of the trees still lay as they fell. Looks like a tree holocaust and so it was.

As you walk along, note the many ohelo bushes with their bright red berries. These are the berries sacred to Madam Pele. You can sample them (just a few; this area is the Nene lunch area) but be sure to toss the first one to the Goddess, as is customary. Otherwise, you might invoke her ire. I'm not kidding!

You may see the endangered Nenes here, having lunch.

Notice also the many small pit craters. I sometimes come here at night, climb down the side of one of the little indentations, spread a blanket out, and watch shooting stars. It's quite comfy; I can lean against the side of the crater, not have to crane my neck, and be out of the wind. It's often very windy here at night.

You'll know when you reach Desolation Peak. Just below it, the cinder road descends back down into the rainforest. This is one of the best places to photograph the entirety of Mauna Loa; that is, if it is not obscured by mist.

On a clear day, you will be able to see Halema'uma'u, Mauna Loa and also Mauna Kea, which will look just like a little bump on the horizon compared to Mauna Loa, Long Mountain. In wintertime, the mountains can be shrouded in a mantle of snow, which is especially majestic. You can also see as far as the Ka'u desert.

Because the weather is so changeable here, the view is always different. Late evening and nighttime viewing can be especially lovely, but do dress warmly. Most nights, the wind picks up and it is quite chilly, if not downright cold. If you're a photographer, you might get some lovely photographs as the light changes in the evening. Mauna Loa turns all silvery, and the stars are lovely.

Now, the hiking way.

Consult the free Park map for the Byron's Ledge route hiking route. There are several trails depending on where you hiking from. **I like to come out of Kilauea Iki Crater and continue on, taking the first path to the left at the top of the steps.** *If you go toward the bench, you are going in the wrong direction.* After about an eighth of a mile, turn left at a path junction, and almost immediately you will see a gate. Go through the gate (close it behind you because of pigs), and then through a lovely forest path carpeted with gold moss, called by locals the Yellow-brick Road.

You can also reach this gate junction by hiking along Byron's Ledge coming from a couple of other places from the Crater Rim trail.

Whichever way you choose, once through the gate, there are several views of Kilauea Caldera that are wonderful. You can stop on Byron's Ledge for great photographs at several places; just follow the not-so-easy-to-discern short paths to the right that go to the edge, **but** *do be careful!!!* There is a real cliffhanger among giant ferns for another spectacular view and photographs of Halema'uma'u, just a few footsteps after going through the gate. *Be cautious!!!*

Continuing on, *keep to the left when you come to the sign which says a portion of the path is closed.* This portion is closed at present, as the sign states.

The terrain changes as you approach the climb up to Desolation Peak, becoming remarkably drier and warmer, until the path itself becomes pure cinder.

Pu'upua'i, the red cinder cone of Kilauea Iki, comes again into sight on your left, but from this vantage point, it appears as a perfect curve of blondish-reddish earth, Pele's Breast. *Please do not try to climb Pu'u Pua'i!*

This whole area was, prior to 1959, a heavily wooded forest area. During the 1959 Kilauea Iki event, prevailing southwest winds blew the molten lava so that the forest on this side was burnt or buried by molten lava. Hot cinders welded themselves together to form "spatter cones." Cinders not as hot were ejected and blown further from the eruption site, cooled down and created the cinder blanket you will walk upon here.

On the path above is the ghostly Desolation Peak, and all around are the bleached white bones of trees and cinder pit craters, just as they were left by Kilauea Iki's eruption of 1959. As you climb the crunchy hill, through 'ohi'a trees sometimes loaded with crimson red lehua blossoms, superb views of Mauna Loa and Mauna Kea arise before your eyes; that is, weather permitting, for sometimes the mountains are blanketed by eerie fog and mist.

To return, retrace your steps to the gate. Instead of turning right after the gate, continue straight ahead until you come to the next junction, about an eighth-mile. You will see a bench. Take a rest and enjoy the magnificent view of Halema'uma'u. To continue on, go back a few steps from the direction you just came from, and you will access the Crater Rim Trail back to Kilauea Iki parking lot. Just climb up, up, and up, and continue straight ahead.

Keanakako'i Crater
(Place of the adze)
Open only to bicyclists and pedestrians.
Suitable for wheel chairs and baby strollers.

This is the BEST vantage point from which to see the eruption. A must see!!!

A portion of Old Crater Rim Drive is now open to foot and bicycle traffic to a point just beyond Keanakako'i Crater. It's about a wonderful two-mile round-trip walk. Park at Devastation Trail parking lot if you are in a car, or, you can hike there. **Continuing from Thurston lava tube, you will see the parking lot at the intersection of Crater Rim Road and Chain of Craters Road, where there is a stop sign.** The parking lot is to your right.

Be forewarned—evening parking is at a premium. Most people want to see the eruption at night. Get there before 5 p.m.

From the parking lot, walk back toward Crater Rim Drive and head west (to your right) past the road barrier onto the closed portion of the road. It's obvious. (The barrier is for vehicle traffic, not pedestrians). You will walk past koa and 'ohi'a forest. Keanakako'i Crater will be to your south. You can't miss it. The road is flat for the most part, paved, and it's an easy walk. You can take a baby stroller or a wheel chair on the road.

Keanakako'i Crater itself is opposite the huge, yawning Kilauea caldera. You won't be able to see much of it at night, but the main attraction is the eruption on the opposite side of the road.

Keanakako'i Crater formed sometime in the 1400's. It was famous throughout the islands for its rare and superior basaltic rock used for making adzes, tools for carving houses and canoes by the kahuna Kako'i (carving experts). However, the crater was covered by a lava flow in 1877 and then again in 1974, so it was once once deeper.

Today the pit crater is 115 feet deep and 1500 feet wide. Some years ago, when Crater Rim Road was completely open, I rode my bike several times a week around the rim, a distance of, according to my calculations, 13 miles. It was a magnificent ride, world-class, through ever changing vistas that took my breath away. I always liked to stop at Keanakako'i Crater and just stand and look and imagine what it was like for the ancients to trek here to this lonely place to dig for basalt.

Drink in the incredible vista below and all around you. If you look closely, during the day you can see a portion of the Crater Rim road that has collapsed into the caldera.

You might see the Nene geese in this area. Please do not feed them. They are safer being wild things!

You might see beautiful titanium lava rocks in this area too during the day. Please do not take them! Leave them for future generations. Besides, once taken, they lose their beautiful rainbow luster.

This is also a safe place to bike, though not a long stretch. Come early in the morning, and you will probably have it all to your self! It's also a great place to come during a full moon. I sometimes come here to view astronomical events, like planetary alignments. Dress warmly if you do—that wind! If you come at night, be sure to bring a flash light.

Note: Another way to view Keanakako'i Crater during the day is to park at either the Devastation Trail parking lot, or, turn left on Chain of Crater Road and park at the one parking place you will see a short distance after you turn. There will be a sign saying Crater Rim Trail. (The trail also continues on your left; take the trail to the right.) You can walk here from the Devastation parking lot in about 8 minutes. From here, you do an easy round trip mile hike to Keanakako'i which meanders through wild grassy areas and across congealed lava. You cannot see the eruption site from here, however. Take water.

Chain of Craters Road

*All mileage given below is measured
from the beginning of Chain of Craters Road.*

Chain of Craters is an 18.8 mile long drive to the sea, with an elevation change of 3700 feet. **It begins 3.3 miles south of the Park Center, at the intersection of Devastation Parking lot.** In 2014, the lava flow from Pu'u O'o began to advance toward Pahoa, which would, if it continued, block the two main access routes for the people of lower Puna. Currently, an emergency access route is being constructed between the Park and Kalapana, along the old route which once connected Kalapana Road before it was inundated with lava.

The Chain of Craters Road is one of the most scenic drives in the world! It's a must do! Down, down, and more down you go, more than 4000 feet to the sea, and all along the way are volcanic wonders. An enormous lava flow in 1995 severed the road that once linked the Park with Kalapana. What goes down must come back up, so at the end of the road, you must turn around and drive back up. It's almost 40 miles round trip. Well worth it!

Make sure you have enough gas! As well as drinking water.

To reach Chain of Craters Road from the entrance to the Park take a left onto Crater Rim Drive just after you pass the Park entrance gate. From the Park Center, take a right. Follow Crater Rim Drive for three miles, past Thurston lava tube, until you reach Devastation Trail. Turn left directly across from the Devastation Trail parking lot at the stop sign. Not hard to find at all. The road is clearly marked.

Get ready for one of the most spectacular drives in your life!

Chain of Craters Road may be one of the most unique experiences you have on the Big Island, or on the planet!

Stretching almost 19 miles and going from 4,000 ft. elevation to sea level, this scenic drive along the East Rift Zone of the volcano is pock-marked with craters of varying shapes and sizes, as well as lava flows, petroglyphs, and, possibly, active lava. Along this road are many interesting hikes, breathtaking vistas, and the opportunity to see the handiwork of Madam Pele.

There are no special facilities or services along the way, other than simple toilets (appropriately named "pit-stops!"). These are located at Mauna Ulu, mile marker 3.6, and at the very end of the road. As I said, gas up before! Come prepared with plenty of drinking water and sunscreen. A hat and good walking shoes are recommended. Of course, rain gear is always handy.

This beautiful and scenic road was begun by local prisoners around 1911. They first constructed a road from the Volcano House to Halema'uma'u and when they successfully completed it, they turned their attention to creating a trail, called Cocketts Trail, named after the construction supervisor (Brownie points!) which ended at Devil's Throat. So that was the beginning of this magnificent world class drive! We owe it to criminals!

Chain of Craters Road proper all the way to the coast was opened in 1965, but it was partially buried during the 1969 Mauna Ulu eruption. It was rebuilt and reopened in 1979. From 1986 to the present, lava has repeated flowed over this road. If you see lava coming, turn around fast!

The road begins in the lush forest, but as you descend, enormous vistas of geologic wonders unroll before your eyes. Many craters, each with their distinctive characteristics, dot the landscape. You may want to stop at a lot of them. Or all of them! Allow a morning or afternoon for a leisurely exploration of every wonderful thing on this drive. Following is an in-depth description.

Place of the Guardians (Pele's Playground)
(Closed but open? Read the full description to see
what I mean)

First stop! Place of the Guardians.
Where is this wonderful place?
Just before and behind Lua Manu Crater, the first
crater along Chain of Craters Road. **There are two ways
to get here.**
In both cases, please take plenty of water. This is a
hike for people with sturdy feet, good hiking shoes, and
good balance. Goats can do very well here also. **It is *not*
suitable for young children and the elderly.
Remember, watch your footing. Be mindful. Eyes on
the ground; no talk when walk!**
**The easiest and safest access is the portion of
Crater Rim Trail just before Lua Manu.**
**To get there, look for the Crater Rim trail head
right after you make the turn on to Chain of Craters
Road. Crater Rim Trail cuts across the highway, less
than an eighth mile after the turn onto Chain of
Craters Road, so look sharp.** You will see a sign on
each side of the road, "Crater Rim Trail." If the trail is
closed, there will be no sign on the right side of the road
and a barricade will be up. There is one parking place on
each side of the road. (You can also park back at
Devastation Trail parking lot, a five minute walk. Or, you
can park at Lua Manu, the next pit crater, just a few
hundred yards down the road, and walk back).
**If you choose to stay on the trail and not divert
into the lava, you will end up at Keanakako'i Crater
overlook.** The whole trail is approximately 0.8 miles to
the overlook.   From here you can see the panoramic
views of Kilauea Caldera and Mauna Loa.
To trek into the lava field, you follow the trail
approximately less than a quarter mile through grassy,
scrubby, beautiful pastel-colored forestland. **Always keep**

your starting point within sight so you don't get lost! I love the delicate golds, silvers and pinks of this place. When you come to the place where you see the congealed lava flow on your left, walk in. In just a few yards, you will be on the flow. There is no path, so you are on your own. *Be careful! Remember—lips closed, eyes on the ground! Lava walking requires concentration.*

The other *always* **accessible way to enter is just to park at Lua Manu pit Crater at 0.5 mile marker and hike behind it.** Again, take care; **there is no path**. You will be walking on what is called shelly lava; it is like walking on seashells, extremely fragile.

This is a place that few people know about. It's really special! However, if you go here, please be very cautious. This is terrain where you can easily sprain an ankle, break a leg, take a very bad fall or get cut badly or worse on the very sharp a'a lava. Basically, this is like walking on glass or razor blades. You need to wear really good footwear, preferably jeans, a hat and take water. **Don't go alone!** !! **Be mindful!!!**

With these warnings, let me describe this incredible place.

Know what a projective test is? It's a personality test designed to let a person respond to ambiguous stimuli, presumably revealing hidden emotions and internal conflicts. An example of such a test is the Rorschach inkblot test. Well, this fantastic landscape is Mother Nature's projective test.

Do you see The Igneous, a strange race of creatures made of living rock and magma, and alien to the eyes of humanity? Do you see Magmaarghs, huge, hideous creatures made of lava who look incredibly deranged, with strange eyes and huge mouths? Do you see Magmion and his hordes of creatures made from charred earth out to destroy and consume the souls of Gore?

Or do you see whimsical, quirky and comical composite beasts such as giant owls, half dolphin-half dog creatures, and perhaps a colossal cookie monster?

Perhaps you see all of the above as you take in this gallery of the imagination, where monsters and other whimsical, fantastic creatures play in a totally surreal landscape? Maybe this strange fantasy-land with its inspired creatures bears the echoes of childhood dreams and nightmares?

Whatever!

You have to admit, Pele had a great time playing here! A real flight of fancy!

This eerie landscape, created by the July 1974 lava flow, is the very best of lava trees and lava tree molds in the Islands, and virtually unknown. You won't find it on Park maps, as far as I know, and I have never found a reference to it in any of the guidebooks.

Shhh!

How did it happen?

Lava moved through a forest of 'ohi'a trees and submerged the lower 3-5 meters of the moist trunks. As the peak flow passed through the area, the surface of the flow subsided, leaving the trunks of trees standing above the new ground surface coated with a skin of solidified lava.

What was left are casts of trees that were in the way of a lava flow. One would think that the trees would have been demolished by the flow, but these lava trees are proof this does not always happen. Lava trees form when lava flows over a forested area and the lava begins to cool around the trees and later burns through to the inside of the trunk. This leaves a hollow mold in the middle of the lava tree, though sometimes part of the charred tree is left over. The inside of the trees show the original texture of the bark. The lava that flowed through the area here must have deflated because the trees are positive features on the landscape instead of holes in the ground.

We know this was a short-lived eruption. The height of the tree molds shows the highest level of lava flow. The direction of flow can be determined using tree molds by observing the seams that form when lava wraps around the tree—the seam is opposite to the direction of flow. Lava trees are formed only by thin flows, but tree molds are preserved in both thin and thick flows. Both structures may indicate the direction of flow of the lava in which they are preserved.

Some of the best formations are toward the back, deeper across the flow. My very favorite is "The Embrace," sometimes called "Tantric Couple." No idea who named these! There are also several circles of formations that remind me of Stonehenge, or prayer circles.

I myself do not come here often; one reason is that I feel it is too dangerous to hike alone, though when I come I usually do come here alone. I love to come on silvery, misty days, but I also like to come on blazing hot afternoons. It's very different.

I do love the ambiance no matter what; I come here in times of personal crisis when I feel I need the special assistance of…The Guardians.

Retrace your steps to the roadway or to your starting point on the trail.

Remember, watch your footing. Be mindful. Eyes on the ground; no talk when walk!.

Continuing on Chain of Craters Road...

Pit craters such as **Lua Manu** (Bird Pit), the first crater on the right side of the road as you descend toward the sea, at the 0.5 marker, and many others along the Chain of Craters Road, formed primarily when lava drained out of chambers beneath the surface, causing the surface to collapse inward to fill the void. These craters are characterized by deep pits with no debris on the rims, indicating a lack of eruptive events in their formation. By the way, "lua" often refers to the toilet in Hawaiian, as in, "He's in the lua."

Most of the pit craters along Chain of Craters Road were formed before written records were kept, but their formation is likely associated with the major subsidence episodes around 1790 that formed much of the modern Kilauea Crater seen today.

Notice the number of bees flying over Lua Manu. Since "manu" means "flying," this could just as well be called "bee pit."

Lua Mani is 330 feet in diameter and 125 feet deep. It formed approximately 200 years ago. During the 1974 eruption, lava filled the crater 50 feet, but two-thirds of it drained back out. You can see on the walls of the crater the high lava mark that was left behind as the lava receded.

Puhimau Crater (Ever-Smoking), is about a half-mile down the road. It is a pit crater that formed between about 1450 and 1800. It is 600 feet wide and about 500 feet deep. Pit Craters, like Puhimau, form when the earth fractures as a volcano shifts or expands. As a volcano erupts, it also settles and cracks develop and migrate upwards. Rocks from the weakened surface dislodge and fall into the cavity. The upward migrating cavity will in time reach the surface and the ground will cave-in. A pit crater forms quickly, shaped like an inverted funnel. Then over time, erosion causes the small opening at the top to grow in size until vertical walls are formed around the edges. You might try singing into this crater; sometimes you can hear your echo. Its name indicates the molten rock is not too far below the surface. No eruptive events have occurred from Puhimau Crater, and no recent historical lava flows have poured into the crater, but sometimes you can see the crater steaming.

Between Puhimau and the next crater, there are acres of dead and dying vegetation on the right side of the road; this is called the Thermal Hotspot. In 1938, this area was about 15 acres large; by 1985, it had increased to 29 acres. Today trees are dying on this side of the road, suggesting an increase in size since 1985. A geochemical study done in 1977 showed higher than usual concentrations of volatile materials, including helium, mercury, carbon dioxide, and various sulphur compounds rising from the ground in the thermal area, suggesting the presence of magma below. It is suspected that the Puhimau Thermal Area, as this area is called, is in the early stages of pit crater formation. That means things are happening here!

It's very beautiful to drive by here in the early morning on cold days when dew is on the ground. Even better it to bicycle by! The grasses are covered with what I can only call hoarfrost. The colors are beautiful.

Ko'oko'olau Crater (named for a medicinal plant) is 1.5 miles down the road. Ko'oko'olau Crater is an excellent example of what happens to a crater after about 200 years of an absence of lava. The crater is completely overgrown with native forest. This is how Kilauea Iki looked before its 1959 eruption. This makes it precarious to walk around the edge. It is also indicative that no thermal activity has occurred here in recent times. This crater formed in a different way than the others along Chain of Craters Road. While most of the other craters formed when the underlying rock gave way, Ko'oko'olau Crater has pumice cones along its rim, suggesting that it was once an eruptive vent.

At approximately mile marker 2.2, across from the Hilina Pali Road, look for a small unmarked pullout on the right. Park and walk across the road to a dirt path. The path leads about 50 feet to the edge of a sheer cliff, which drops off into the abyss. This massive 150 ft. wide by 165 ft. deep crater is called **Devil's Throat**, appropriately named!

Devil's Throat! You are on your own, so take care—**there are no guardrails to block you so very carefully step around** the crumbling edges of the pit. It was formed in early 1912. It's very deep with vertical walls. It's rumored that this is where law enforcement dispose of confiscated pot plants! Or used to. Not potted plants—pot plants!

Park rangers discourage tourists from visiting this crater (They have their reasons?); a *Danger No Entry* sign is posted just before the crater rim. Or was.

One of the reasons is that one comes upon the rim of the crater without any warning! There is no warning, no sigh posted, no nothing, at least the last time I was there. **Do not let children loose here! Or animals! Do not come here intoxicated! Do not come in the dark or in the fog! If you fall in, you are dead!**

The hike itself is only about a 50 foot trail. The ground around the crater is very fractured and disintegrating, and the cliff edges periodically collapse. **Be wary of strong winds that might push you into the crater.**

As of now there is no known historical Native Hawaiian name for Devil's Throat. It was first described in 1909, which means probably that this pit crater formed some time at the end of the 19th century. Early descriptions indicate that the opening was once much narrower, hence the "throat" resemblance. Since then, the overarching ceiling has collapsed.

The U.S. Geological Survey calls this crater "the best, most obvious example of a collapse crater at Kilauea and one of the best in the world."

The best time for viewing as well as photography is at high noon or thereabouts, when the bottom of the crater and the walls are not in shadow.

The Devil's Throat. Dangerous! Exciting!
Be careful!

Hilina Pali Road
Hilina Pali Road is open as far as Kulanaokuaiki
Campground to vehicle traffic, and to foot traffic and
bicycles beyond. Kulanaokuaiki campground is also open
for camping.

**At approximately 2.2 miles down Chain of
Craters, on the right, is the Hilina Pali Road. If you
are just doing the Chain of Craters drive, no need to
stop here.**

Hilina pali means "windy cliff." Few tourists go
here. **Four wheel drive vehicles are best, as you will
find out.** This narrow, one-lane, rough nine-mile paved
road ends at Hilina Pali Lookout. **This is a day trip on its
own, if you have four-wheel drive. Or an overnight
camping excursion. This trail requires planning.**
Check at the Park Center for conditions.

Do this drive on a sunny day. Heavy rain may cause
flooding. Set your odometer at the top of the road.

The Hilina Pali Road starts through scrub with
scattered trees of 'ohi'a and koa. After a stretch of
pahoehoe lava, vegetation varies greatly, from open scrub
forest to desert. You will pass the Mauna Iki trail head,
and the Kulanaokuaiki Campground, and then come to a
former campground, now closed for Nene protection,
Kipuka Nene. This is an area of open and closed forest of
'ohi'a trees, spared by recent lava flows. Beyond is
another area of pahoehoe lava desert, then another forested
kipuka, then lava desert again. After this, on rather older
lava, is a savanna. You will pass another kipuka and then
the road ends at Hilina Pali, a great fault scarp 450 m high.
This is part of the semi-arid Ka'u desert. This is the
general description.

Specifically, at the 0.9 mile marker, there is cliff on
the left, the Koa'e fault system, which lies between the
east and southwest rift zones. The lava flow here is
approximately 650 years old, but the fault itself, a reverse

92

fault, which means it is lower on the side facing away from the ocean, defines a slippage between the northern and southern parts of Kilauea. Koa'e fault is 10 miles long, 1.5 miles wide and 50 feet high, approximately.

At the 3.5 mile marker you reach Kulanaokuaiki Campground, at 2700-feet elevation. There is no water and little shade. There are nine campsites; two of these sites are wheelchair accessible. There is a toilet (no running water), and picnic tables. Fires and pets are not permitted. First come, first serve. You pay by putting your money in the box, ten dollars per night, with a maximum stay of seven nights. Seniors and Golden Access folks are only five dollars a night. There is a 911 telephone here.

Kulanaokuaiki means *shaking of a sharp ridge,* or literally, *little trembling spine*, and is named for the Koa'e Fault that is visible from the campground. The camp itself sits between a 1,300 year old lava flow and a younger 650 year old flow.

Just beyond the camp ground, at the 3.8 mile marker, the road goes up and over Koa'e fault. There is a parking spot here and a sign for Mauna Iki. You can park and explore the fault. The big boulders reveal how active the ground is here. The Mauna Iki trail begins here and traverses the Ka'u desert to Footprints Trail, which is described later. The trail to Footprints (at Highway 11) is 8.8 miles through usually hot desert. So you need to plan for this one.

At odometer 5.2, you arrive at Kipuka Nene. Nene are of course the endangered wild geese. Kipuka Nene used to be the Hilina campground, but to protect the birds which started nesting here, the campground was moved to Kulanaokuaiki,

The tree with the yellow flower and long seed pod is the Mamane, the main food source for the endangered Palila bird, a Hawaiian Honeycreeper. It also nests in the tree. If the tree goes, the birds go. The Mamane was an

93

important tree resource and had a number of uses in ancient Hawaii.

At odometer 5.4 there is a trail on the left. It's used by horse riders and mountain bikers who are in the know.

The road ends on the rift at odometer 8.6. The view from here is stupendous. Almost 2300 feet above sea level, you can see the Ka'u desert ending at the beautiful sea.

An extensive trail system begins here, all of which are multi-day excursions and require planning and registering with the Park.

You can take the trail furthest to the left and in about 30 feet there is a stone marker with arrows pointing to Puna, Amua Point, Pu'u Ka Pukapu, Kalue, South and Ka'u. Below this is a stone which is a remembrance to honor those killed when Hilina Pali dropped into the ocean during a 7.2 earthquake and generated a 48 foot tsunami.

The other trails are marked with signs and short descriptions of the Park's back country.

Briefly, the two trails continue, one down the hill to the coast, and another into the desert, along the top of the cliff. There is a shelter with a water catchment system. There is a small cairn north of the shelter that marks an interesting freshwater crack where you can take a refreshing dip.

The other trail is the Mauna Iki trail (9.6 level miles round trip). It leads through meadow lands to a cabin at Kipuka Pepeiao where there is also water. The downhill trail switchbacks steeply down to the coast to Ka'aha Point, about 8 miles round trip. Located 7.7 miles from the nearest trail head, the Halape Campsite offers a small sandy beach where hikers can camp under the coconut trees.

Check with rangers at the Park Center for current information on this trail, if you want to take it. To repeat, **these excursions require careful planning and equipment, as well as Park registration**. Here is the

Park link for more information on back country hiking and maps:
https://www.nps.gov/havo/planyourvisit/hike_bc.htm.

Fun no? Turn around now and head back in the direction from which you came, savoring your back country experience.

Continuing on Chain of Craters Road...

Hi'iaka Crater (the Sister of Pele), about 2.4 miles along Chain of Craters, is a small collapse pit, formed in 1968 and was further modified in 1973 by lava that flowed from both nearby vents. There are some interesting features around the crater. For example, there are some tree molds near by, and if you walk about 300 feet to the southwest, you will see the Koa'e fault scarp, which acted as a dam to lava flows pouring out of Hi'iaka Crater in 1973.

Pauahi Crater is located 3.3 miles along Chain of Craters Road. Pauahi Crater actually consists of three overlapping prehistoric pit craters. These craters cut across prehistoric lava flows and ash layers roughly 350-500 years old. Pauahi was active as recently as 1979.

Pauahi means *the fire is out*. *Pau* means out, and *ahi* means fire. Just for your information, *pau* is a good Hawaiian word to know, and it was the first word I learned after aloha and mahalo. For example, if you are having dinner and someone invites you to have more, you can say, "Thank you, I'm pau." or, "Mahalo, all pau!" *Pau hana* means chill out time, time for enjoyment, relaxation. *Pau hana Friday* means Friday, the end of the work week. You get the drift.

Pauahi is about 1600 feet long, 330 feet wide, and 500 feet deep. Three eruptions have occurred near Pauahi Crater in historical times, in 1973 and 1979. The November 1973 eruption lasted a total of 31 days. Two fissures opened within minutes of each other, and lava began to pool in both the east and west pits of the crater. The lava flowed in from the fissures, also erupting from the crater itself, creating a huge lava lake at the bottom of the crater. The November 1979 eruption lasted only one day and was preceded by a number of small earthquakes. During the peak of the earthquake swarm, as many as 20 earthquakes per hour shook the ground beneath the Pauahi Crater area.

This is not one of the most dramatic craters, but if you walk around a bit, you might find interesting geological artifacts—Pele's hair, palagonite, which is a yellow clay, Pele's tears, etc. Look and enjoy, but then leave them in place. With millions of visitors each year, if everyone took something, well...you know.

Pauahi is culturally important; you may see ho'okupu offering, sometimes wrapped in pū'olo, ti leaves. Be respectful.

Coming up are two of my favorite places, **Pu'u Huluhulu and Mauna Ulu**. Continue on Chain of Craters. Take the road to the left, clearly marked, 3.7 miles down the road. **This is a must see.** This is also the place to access the Napau Crater trail head.

Pu'u Huluhulu
Shaggy Hill
A must see!

First, there are restrooms here!
Pu'u Huluhulu is a cinder and spatter cone that was
built by eruptions about 300 to 400 years ago. Pu'u
Huluhulu is a *kipuka*, a place where lava has flowed all
around but left a swath of island unscathed. Think *forest
island*. At this kipuka, especially early in the morning,
many rare forest birds may be seen and heard. On a clear
day, the view is unsurpassed in the islands—you can see
Mauna Loa, Mauna Kea, Pu'u 'O'o and the Pacific Ocean.
The trail, if you want to walk it (**highly recommended**), is
a 2.5-mile round trip course over lava rock (wear proper
shoes) and then up the cone. This is an easy to moderate
hike, but with a steep quarter-mile climb up the cone. The
trail head is about 100 yards from the parking area, and is
marked by ahu, stacked rocks. Marked, but slightly subtle,
so pay attention.

You'll hike across the lonely a'a lava flow, through
spatter ramparts, fissures and lava tree molds. The lava
tree molds are very interesting. Take time to look down
into them. Hawaiian mythology tells how Pele, in a fit of
rage after losing a sled race with a chief of Puna, chased
him in the form of lave, overrunning people and turning
them to pillars of stone. No wonder they seem so... sad!

I always feel an affinity for the straggly 'ohi'a trees
and lava tree molds on each side of the path, which seem
like sad and alien creatures stranded in a forbidding world.
Mauna Ulu, "Growing Mountain," can be seen in the
distance, a tall, still-steaming, shield-shaped red mountain
formed by numerous fierce eruptions along the volcanic
rift zone just a few years ago.

Walk carefully as the lava ramparts here are sharp as
razor blades. You will come to a field of pahoehoe lava,
as smooth as the a'a was rough. Then you will hike up

through a forested area, the kipuka, to Pu'u Huluhulu itself, a verdant oasis where lava has flowed all around but left this swath of land unscathed. The trail is narrow and steep, and switches-back eleven times before reaching the top.

Just before reaching the very top, if you watch carefully, you will see a short trail to the right. This is a good place to sit in the soft grass for a while and stare at Mauna Ulu. This is a nice spot for lunch or a snack, or also a wonderful place to meditate.

Then continue up to the top. It's usually very windy up here, and chilly, so remember to take a parka or jacket. Especially in the evening. There's a marker pointed in various directions to the different landmarks. I love to sit and stare at Mauna Ulu from this vantage point.

Here is a magnificent 360 degree view, if it is clear. Puu O'o, on a clear day, may be seen smoking and belching away, and sometimes you can faintly see the glow of the red molten lava that wounds down from O'o's flanks to the sea thirty miles away. Directly opposite to it, and much nearer, is Halema'uma'u, with its toxic plume rising majestically high into the sky. In early morning sunlight, it is colored light hues of orange, pink and blue. The peaks of Mauna Kea and Mauna Loa may be clear; massive Mauna Loa, "Long Mountain," the second largest mountain in the solar system (the largest is on Mars), looms across the Island from the north to the south like a colossal sleeping giant, and the tip of Mauna Kea can be shrouded in snow. You may see all the way across the Ka'u desert to the furthest tip of the Island, South Point, if it is a clear day. Since hiking Mauna Ulu is now prohibited, this is a good place to sit and read my description of Mauna Ulu below in the next section. You can at least experience the thrill vicariously.

Looking straight down, peer into the heart of the cinder and spatter cone that was built by eruptions about 300 or more years ago. Birds twitter and fly from branches of trees that line the steep and inaccessible walls of the pit crater that has been spared the rivers of lava that have overrun the rest of the surrounding country. Look out over the frozen lava plain at the base of Pu'u Huluhulu, and you can see the now the stunning and forbidding-looking remains of a huge lava pond surrounded on all sides by a wall of lava twenty feet taller than the lake. When it erupted only forty years ago, it sent huge quantities of molten lava flowing in all directions, all the way to the ocean. Violent earthquakes rocked this area and a miles-long fissure opened, with fountaining over 200 feet in the air.

I love to sit and stare at Mauna Ulu. (Haven't I already told you that?) With the sunlight striking it, the heavy iron content of Mauna Ulu glows surreally red, and the incredible lava formations—escarpments and crevices and crags—appear like a stone citadel, made up of ornate and strangely decorated palaces and temples with giant walls, terraces and ramps. Sculptures and fantasies seem carved into ebony rock, and the frozen rivers and riverlettes of black lava seem still to course down the slopes, creating at one place a huge lake with its still frozen waves.

Return back the way you came. **There is another short trail with fascinating lava formations that begins in the parking lot. Look for the sign that points to the opposite direction from Puu Huluhulu. It's really worth it to take ten minutes and explore.** Besides the fantastic formations and colors, this is where the 1969 fissure opened up.

Mauna Ulu (Growing Mountain)
(Closed for hiking at present but views are free!)

Unfortunately hiking Mauna Ulu is not an option presently; it never was encouraged by the Park but until the 2018 eruption it was not prohibited. It has always been one of my favorite places to explore, precisely because it is a place for the adventurous, but please experience it vicariously in my description here, written before it exploring was prohibited.

Take extreme caution in exploring Mauna Ulu. Wear appropriate footwear, take lots of water, and tread carefully!!! You are on your own out here. Sometimes there are no visitors around anywhere; they can't hear you if you get into trouble, and your cell phone may not work! Mine didn't the last time I was there. **Park Rangers will not encourage you to explore Mauna Ulu alone, and you should never go alone.** At the very least, let someone know where you have gone, and report back to them after hiking to let them you know you are safe.

With that cautionary advice, I will say that that I hike Mauna Ulu often;it's one of my fave hikes, but I always take great care!

The Mauna Ulu eruption of Kilauea began on May 24, 1969, and ended on July 22, 1974. At the time, Mauna Ulu was the longest flank eruption of any Hawaiian volcano in recorded history. The eruption created a new vent, covered massive amounts of land with lava, and added new land to the island. Mauna Ulu fountained 1770 feet, only second to Kilauea Iki's record-making 1900 feet. From 1969 to 1974 the Mauna Ulu lava flows covered 40 square miles, traveled 7 miles to the coast and covered several areas with 25 feet of lava. Molten lava streamed down the 700 feet high Holei Pali cliffs, which are on down the Chain of Crater Road. It buried roads and cultural sites as well as made new land. It covered or partially filled five pit craters, including 'Alo'i Crater and 'Alae Crater, the latter spectacularly filled when a huge lava fall, higher and wider than the American Falls at Niagara. cascaded into it. Ejecta from the fountaining in the form of cinder, Pele' tears, reticulite and Pele's hair rained down upon the forests, creating fires. It created 150 acres of new land.

By early 1970 the Mauna Ulu lava shield was being created during lulls in activity as the surface lava cooled. But at the summit, the large crater was a roiling lake of molten lava. It must have been an incredible sight, as the lava circulated round and round and fountains danced. In fact, a platform was built to allow viewing of the incredible spectacle, but one morning, it was discovered that the platform was missing, and so was a part of the crater's walls, all collapsed into the red-hot cauldron during the night!

For the next almost five years, Mauna Ulu grew to 400 feet tall, as thin sheets of lave flowed over previous layers and cooled and hardened. After the eruption, in the summer of 1974, the molten lava receded from Mauna Ulu's crater. Show was over. Pau!

For a while.

Pele creates, Pele destroys.

There is no real trail to the top of Mauna Ulu! The slope is gentle but the lava is extremely fragile; several times, my feet have broken through some of the many shallow lava tubes. Listen carefully for the sound of hollow areas as you take each step; this area is famous for broken ankles, arms and legs. The ground crunches as you carefully step along the shell lava, often the only sound to be heard in the stillness of this lava plain.

Steam and smoke are still coming out of the ground all around. You may choose to hike up through the huge channel where once a river of molten lava poured. The stinky smell of sulphur, like rotten eggs, becomes noticeable.

Finally, you will reach the top of the cone. Stop well before approaching the pit itself. You can see for miles in every direction, all the way to the sea. Black congealed lava spreads out for miles and glistens like black diamonds in the sunlight.

A huge crack completely around the summit of the cone, about ten feet from the edge, looks like it might break and collapse into the pit at any minute! What is at the bottom of that pit, and how far down it goes, no one knows, (ha, ha) for the sides of the pit, almost a perfect circle, drop 180 degrees straight down into a blackness from which smoke unendingly spews in light wisps. Even hovering helicopters have been unable to photograph what is in the bottom of the pit, or if there is even a bottom (Not sure about that, but it makes a good story! And in fact, I did make a good story about it, a true story—"The Caldera," which you can read in my book *The Cry Room*). My heart pounds just to think of falling into that dark unknown.

I usually hike around counter-clockwise, as if I am circumambulating the Kaaba Stone. Carefully, very carefully, skirt the threatening great crack!

Approach the edge at your own risk!

Like Devil's Throat, the edge is crumbly, and a small earthquake or gust of wind or even a hiccup could take one over. I do not advise trying to peer over the edge.

Admire the lava, which takes on a variety of hues— bright reds, browns, tans, grays, and blues. Great lava channels cut into the ground, and you will have to jump across some and scramble up and down others. *Be careful!*

As you approach the other side of the cone, the scene completely changes! The jutted and razor-sharp turrets and spires of lava become flowing, swirling motifs and gingerbread gewgaws and fantastic giant imaginary animals. The graceful pahoehoe lava formations seem as if they are oddly frozen musical notations of some kind, and there is a hallucinatory power to the landscape, a Disneyland of frozen magma.

Make your way cautiously down again.

Congratulations! You have just had a most extraordinary experience!

Even if only vicariously!

Napau Trail

Napau trail requires a permit. You can inquire here: **https://www.nps.gov/havo/planyourvisit/hike_bc.htm**.

This is a challenging 14-mile round trip trail. If you arrange a car at the end of the trail, or a ride, you shorten the trip by 7 miles! There is a parking pull-out on the Chain of Craters Road. A permit and planning is required for camping. Rangers recommend a stock of at least three quarts of water per day for the hike. This trail is not suitable for small children. Cell phones do not get reception. Get a backcountry free map from the Park center. Check in with the rangers to let them know you are out there.

This is a very dynamic, volcanically active area, erupting as recently as early winter 2011. That's recent! It can erupt again at any minute!

You will trek over congealed lava rivers and channels, pass lava trees, look down into pit craters, stroll through forests—in short, have a wonderful time.

For general information, the trail begins at the Mauna Ulu parking lot. Follow the trail to Puu Huluhulu and from there, follow the ahu, the rock piles, and stay on the trail. Watch your footing! The journey to Napau is seven miles one way over wild and truly fascinating landscape. Remember to keep your eyes on the ground as you walk. The trail skirts around the mouth of Makaopuhi Crater and eventually ends at Napau Camp, which has no water or shelter.

More specifically, the trail continues from the bottom of Pu'u Huluhulu, and it is clearly marked. It passes under a "perch pond" on Mauna Ulu's side. After crossing Pu'u Huluhulu, it travels along the bed of a lava channel.

A strenuous three-mile trek across the desert passes an impressive rift from the Mauna Ulu eruption. Here you can see a good example of the start of a lava tube, before reaching the immense Makaopuhi Crater.

Then you will hike up the 'Alae Shield, near the rim of the peak crater. The trail climbs down the 'Alae Shield and reaches Makaopuhi Crater in about 2.2 miles. From here, the trail travels through rainforest. The 500 year-old double crater is the largest in the east rift zone, and erupted in 1922, 1965, and 1972, The trail here begins to skirt the crater and enters a dense and beautiful rainforest. This area was covered by lava in 1840. Pass through the sometimes dense rainforest toward the old Pulu factory.

There are the remains of an old pulu station at Napau. Pulu is the soft, downy material that grows on the fronds and fiddleheads of the hapu'u fern. In the late 1800's, a market for the material to be used in pillow and mattresses flourished. The Napau factory processed pulu from 1851 – 1884, but then it was discovered that in dry climates, the pulu became dust! Hence, the end of what was thought a good idea. Actually, it turned out great. Our forests of hapu'u would have been destroyed, as the koa industry destroyed the great koa forests.

Pulu harvesting was labor intensive. First the stalk was cut with a stone too, then the pulu was removed with a bone scraper and collected in bags. Fires nearby dried the pulu. Each tree fern produced only five ounces of material; a mattress required 30 pounds!

It is believed by archaeologists that over-harvesting caused the industry to fail, and this station was abandoned around 1867. It was forgotten, and rediscovered by a scientist fairly recently. You can still see the walls.

.You can read about it in detail here: https://www.nps.gov/havo/learn/historyculture/pulu-factories.htm

P. S. Pulu was used and is still used by the Hawaiians as a wound poultice. It is believed to have antiseptic qualities. I have used it myself in lieu of a band-aid when getting cuts while hiking in the forest.

After exploring the old factory a bit, you will continue on through 'ohi'a trees and tree ferns in the forest; the rainforest will sometimes open up at places where lava has burned down the trees.

As you skirt around the west and then south side of Makaopuhi Crater, the path enters a forest of uluhe (false-staghorn fern), hapu'u and 'ohi'a trees, becoming more defined. Pleasant trekking through the forest, surrounded by twittering birds, gives some welcome shade from what can be piercing heat.

Pass the Kalapana trail on the right, and follow the main route as it swings gently northeast; it continues as a clearly defined trail through the forest. In three miles you come to a junction. Straight on (left) takes you further towards Pu'u 'O'o; at this time, this trail is closed. Take the right fork and you come to a dead end, the edge of the Napau Crater. A small clearing on the crater rim looks out across the crater with a great view of smoking Pu'u 'O'o. This overlook makes for a great lunch spot before returning by reverse route.

This is a day trek that requires some planning and preparation, but for the seasoned hiker, it's fab!
You can read more about it here: https://www.nps.gov/havo/planyourvisit/hike_napau.htm

Continuing on Chain of Craters...

Ainahou Ranch

(Ainahou Ranch is a hit or miss. Sometimes open, sometimes closed., depending upon if the Nenes are nesting. Mostly closed. Ask at the Visitor Center.)

At mile 4.1 is the 13.3 acre **Ainahou Ranch**, built in 1941 and listed on the National Register of Historic Places. This is one of my favorite places! However, check with the rangers to find out if is it open. **It is closed more often than not,** due to the Nene breeding cycle. If it is open, you are in for a real treat, but you must hike a bit. Please remember it is illegal to approach or disturb the endangered Nene in any way. Also, be wary of pigs—do not approach them if you should see them.

At approximately 4.2 miles you will see a sign and a right hand turn for the ranch. Make the right turn and you will come to a locked gate. Park off the road as much as you can. After you have parked your car, walk around the gate and simply go down the road. This is an easy walk approx. 2.7 miles one way. The ranch itself is not marked on the trail other than the sign on Chain of Craters Road showing the turnoff for the ranch,

After approximately one-half mile, you will encounter a split in the road. A trail sign tells you to take the left—the sign is *wrong*. Do *not* take the left fork; instead, take the right fork.

After having taken the *right* fork, you are now headed towards the ranch, which is still not visible. To the front and to the right of you are tall fir trees; these firs mark the start of the ranch itself. Keep along this road until you see another road branching to the right. Take this right branch and keep going. You are now entering the fir tree area. Round the curve and you will see the ranch.

This incredible ranch was built by H. C. Shipman as a haven against Japanese invasion during WWII. Shipman was very interested in wildlife conservation and one of the uses for the ranch was to provide protection for the endangered Nene. Shipman was a cattle rancher—the original property was over 64,000 acres of pristine native forests and grasslands. The property is still home to Nene and is not open to the public during the breeding season if Nenes are found to be nesting in the area, most of the time.

The 13.3-acre historic site sits within a native mesic forest at an elevation of 3000 feet. Within this forest, gardens surround a unique house creating an exotic setting that reflects Shipman's love of horticulture. He grew a vast collection of plants, which included orchids, orchards, a tree farm, and rare plants from around the world.

In 1971, Shipman terminated his lease with B. P. Bishop Estate, at which point the National Park Service acquired it.

When you are ready to leave this lovely place, just retrace your path.

Back on Chain of Craters Road...

Muliwai a Pele, R*ivers of Pele,* is about 7.4 miles down Chain of Craters Road. It is a lava channel located on the top of Holei Pali escarpment. The lava channel formed in 1974 during the eruption of Mauna Ulu. Pahoehoe lava flowed from Mauna Ulu, which we just visited. This viewpoint overlooks lava flows from 1969 and the 1969-74 eruptions from Mauna Ulu. Here the lava descends Holei Pali, a 1300 feet escarpment along the Hilina fault system. and continues towards the sea. The 1969 flow did not quite reach the sea, but the later flows did. Holei Pali is a 1300 feet high escarpment along the Hilina fault system. You can get a great look at it at mile marker 14.4, described below.

Kealakomo lookout is about 9.9 miles down Chain of Craters Road. Kealakomo means T*he Entrance Path,* an appropriate name for the panoramic view of the ocean and the vast lava field that covered the ancient village of Kealakomo. Stop and be amazed!

A wooden deck perched on the side of the cliff will come into view. The handicapped-accessible Kealakomo is built on the Holei Pali and looks down over a 2,000 ft. drop to the ocean. The Holei Pali is a fault escarpment which has moved downward relative to the east rift zone. During the earthquakes of 1868, and 1975, the last major movement of these cliffs occurred.

The deck faces the direction of Kealakomo Village, destroyed in a 1971 lava flow. The coastal village was abandoned after the 1868 earthquake and tsunami and buried during the Mauna Ulu flows. Notice the dull black ribbons of lava—these are 'a'a lava flows of 1969-1974. The silvery ribbons are pahoehoe lava.

This can be a great place for lunch, though usually it is windy. The Naulu Trail begins across the street. It eventually connects with the Napau Crater Trail to the north. It also intersects the un-maintained 10-hour Kalapana trail.

The pullout at **Halona Kahakai** is very near the crest of the Holei Pali fault escarpment. *The road takes a dramatic hairpin turn that you should approach with caution.*

For a little lesson in volcanoes, when the kind of lava that built Kilauea cools, slopes rarely exceed a six per-cent grade. Steeper land forms, such as the cliffs of Holei Pali, which you can see from Halona Kahakai, were formed by faulting or erosion. The lava plain below has broken off and dropped from the main slope. Again, notice the two types of lava, 'a'a and pahoehoe.

In another mile, the elevation will have dropped to 1,000 ft as you rapidly approach the coast.

For several hundred feet above and below **Alanui Kahiko** (Old Road) lookout, at approx. mile marker 13.7, can be seen remnants of the old Chain of Craters Road, buried under 300 feet of lava in the 1972 eruptions of 'Alae Lava shield flow. Walk *ma kai* (toward the sea) about 100 feet to see it.

To take in fully the enormous power of the volcano that you are driving on, pull over at mile marker 14.4, **the Holei Pali overlook.** It is easy to see how the lava came pouring down in waves over the Holei Pali, forming gigantic rivers flowing down the Pali, and oozing its way to the ocean. Holei Pali (*Pali* means cliff) is the name of the 400-meter high escarpment along the Hilina fault system. Lava flowed from Mauna Ulu over the cliffs between 1969 and 1974. Whew!

At mile 14.9, to the left, is the **Skylights Climb**, a trail that leads up to a 30-40 foot hill with a hole in it—the lava tube tumulus (mound)—where magma was once vented. This lava tube is usually overlooked. It is right off the road. Lot's of Pele hair here. Remember, leave it where you find it!

Pu'uloa, at approx. mile marker 16.3, is the largest concentration of ancient Hawaiian stone carvings in the State, perhaps in Polynesia, with more than 20,000 petroglyphs. Once you reach mile marker 16.3 you'll see two pullouts on either side of the road and a small park sign marking the start of the seven-tenths of a mile petroglyph trail. **This is a must stop!**

Pu'uloa Petroglyphs
A must!

Pu'uloa means "*long hill*," but it also has a hidden meaning, a *kaona*, "*Hill of Long Life*." It is a sacred place to the Hawaiians, and especially to the people of Kalapana. The archaeological site of Pu'uloa contains over 23,000 petroglyph images!

Geologically, Pu'uloa is a volcanic dome with outlying areas of ancient, relatively level pahoehoe lava fields dated between AD 1200-1450. Perfect for a sort of canvas! Or diary! Or genealogical chart!

The walk to Pu'uloa (1.5 miles round trip) takes you over an ancient field of pahoehoe lava with small scrubby plants pushing their way between the cracks. The path is well worn and marked by cairns of rock, *ahu,* as well as by its smoothness and discolorations, for untold numbers of feet have trod over this path for centuries. The Park has built a boardwalk around some of the petroglyphs to protect the fragile carvings while still allowing visitors to enjoy them.

In Hawaiian, the petroglyphs are called *ki'i pohaku*, stone images. Their meaning is apparently lost, which seems to indicate that they are very ancient indeed. They are dated between 1200-1450 A. D.

William Ellis, a missionary to the Hawaiian and Society Islands, recorded the earliest written observation of the petroglyphs at Pu'uloa in 1823. According to his informants, the glyphs were a sort of travelogue.

He wrote: "When there were a number of concentric circles with a dot or mark in the center, the dot signified a man, and the number of rings denoted the number in the party who had circumambulated the island. When there was a ring and a number of marks, it denoted the same; the number of marks showing of how many the party consisted; and the ring, that they had traveled completely around the island; but when there was only a semicircle, it

113

denoted that they had returned after reaching the place where it was made."

Hmm.

Anthropologist Martha Beckwith visited the site in 1914 and wrote: "Rode out to Puuloa on the line between Kealakomo and Apuki. Here is a large pahoehoe mound used as a depository for the umbilical cord at the birth of a child. A hole is made in the hard crust, the cord is put in and as stone is placed over it. In the morning the cord has disappeared; there is no trace of it. This insures long life for the child. Mrs. Kama, born in 1862, was a native of Kamoamoa. Her mother brought her cord there. She had 15 children and for each one at birth the visit was made to Puuloa. Another mound, on the southern boundary of Apukiu., called Puumanawalea, was similarly used….Puuloa is especially rich. There are holes, pictures, initials chiseled into the rock."

She further interpreted some of the symbols as follows:
A dot symbolized the hole for a child.
A dot in a circle represented the hole for the first born.
A dot with two circles meant the first born of an ali'i, a chief.
A plain circle symbolized a calabash.
A jagged line was a mo'o, a lizard.
A circle with a long line was a puloulou, a tapa covered ball on a stick carried by an ali'i, a symbol of taboo.
A cross with a dot at each end was a cross before a chief at night in traveling.

Interestingly, petroglyphs do not occur throughout Polynesia. According to one authority, a line drawn from Hawaii to New Zealand divides the islands into those that have the strange drawings and those that do not—those east of the line are the isles with petroglyphs. This then, might indicate that their origin lies southeast, toward

Easter Island, where petroglyphs and a written language existed prehistorically. Lots of room for conjecture here!

The petroglyphs consist of straight lines, semicircles, and concentric rings as well as strange stick figures of humans that are very powerfully emotive. There are also thousands of small pits drilled into the lava—it is commonly believed that the umbilical cords of newborn infants were buried here as a sacred practice, just as Mrs. Kama said.

There are also some who believe that the mysterious symbols are a form of divine communion known only by the kahunas, the priests. Still others believe that the petroglyph fields were genealogical record repositories. I have stood and looked at the petroglyphs of Pu'uloa for hours, and whatever they are, they are certainly some kind of sacred record keeping. This is a place of *mana*, spiritual power. **Do tread respectfully.**

Interestingly, most of the human figures are males, but some of the groupings are obviously made of a man, woman, and child. Many of the figures are warrior figures; their helmets and weapons are clearly discernible, and their fighting stances are definitely intimidating. There are also drawings of canoes, fish, and lizards, and more rarely, symbols that seem to be the sun, moon and stars. I have never seen petroglyphs of flowers, which indicates to me that there is definitely something intrinsically masculine about the symbols. I think they were drawn by men. Wouldn't women draw flowers?

It is forbidden by law to disturb the petroglyphs in any way. Please do not touch them or make rubbings. If the great rivers of lava of Goddess Pele have flowed all around them and spared them, certainly we can too. With that admonition, I will tell you about the petroglyphs that lie just on the other side of the small hill off the far side of the boardwalk.

Walk in a two o'clock direction from the boardwalk over the hill. You will be amazed and delighted by the thousands of petroglyphs! Please tread lightly and very respectfully if you explore them; do not walk on them. Look up at the immense pali (cliff), with its broad, frozen rivers of lava, and then down again at the inexplicable stick drawings. You may get, as I do, a strange feeling for the sacredness of this spot and the mana, the power, it must have held for the ancients—a place where the indomitable forces of nature meet with the mind of man.

I like to meditate here during the intense heat of the day. What do I meditate upon? The puniness but courage of striving humankind in the face of the overwhelming forces of nature.

Be sure and bring lots of water if you do come here in the midday. It can be really hot! Also good walking shoes are a must. Sunglasses too!

Take a moment to stand back and look up at the pali (the cliffs). Imagine what it would be like to come here and carve the symbol of your life, your genealogy, in the lava with a primitive tool. Enjoy your goosebumps!

Continuing on Chain of Craters Road...

Holei Sea Arch
(Currently closed)

Near the end of Chain of Craters Road is the Holei Sea Arch. (Mile marker 18.8). Actually, it may or may not be there—it just took a big hit in the July 2022 storms.

The original sea arch viewing area has been closed because of cracks and instability in the coastal cliffs in the area. The new viewing area is located about 1,000 feet past the gate at the end of Chain of Craters Road, atop hardened pahoehoe lava. It is set back away from the cliff edge, and is marked with orange stanchions and rope. Parking is available on either side of the road.

Extreme caution—keep away from the dangerous cliff edges!

The Holei Sea Arch is 90 feet high and was created about 550 years ago. Sea arches are formed when lava is continuously pounded by heavy surf until it is undercut in the shape of an arch. The term for the creation of this sea arch is "differential erosion", which is the difference in the hardness of various layers of lava flow. Sea arches can be found along much of the southern coastline of Hawai'i.

The cliffs are 80 to 90 feet high, but many waves still spray and wash over them, so use caution. Restrooms are available; well, let's call them, appropriately enough, "pit-stops."

Until just a few years ago, great molten rivers of fire coursed down the slopes of the Pali and cascaded into the sea here. At that time, every night hundreds of tourists parked here and walked out onto the lava fields to watch the hair-raising sight. The really intrepid ventured close enough to the molten lava to burn the soles of their shoes.

Sea arches like Holei remind us of the ephemeralness of all things. For as soon as they are born, created, they begin to die, disintegrate. Wind and water begin to erode them, just as the elements act upon all things to transform them into something else.

It was within sight of the Holei Sea Arch that my friend, noted photographer Prem Nagar, fell into the sea of fire when an earthquake broke off the lava shelf upon which he was standing. His last words were, according to his friend who ran for dear life when he felt the quake, and survived, "Give me a show, mama."

She did.

Pau!
The End.

This is the end of Chain of Craters Road. In 2014, construction began to provide an emergency access route between the Park and Kalapana, in case lower Puna becomes inundated with lava. You can view the end of the rode by walking 0.5 mile from the Holei Sea Arch parking area.

Now, turn around, drive slowly, and take the time to admire and appreciate the majesty of this incredible place, as you drive the 18.8 miles back to the beginning of Chain of Craters Road.

What a trip!

A world-class drive!

A Hidden Place Within the Park (Shhh!)...
Pua Po'o
(Cock's Comb Cave, The Wild Cave)

Currently unavailable. Call for up-to-date info.

Call for information 808-985-7373; times are variable and reservations are required. This program is administered by Friends of Hawai'i Volcanoes National Park. Check their website here for updates and other interesting info: https://www.fhvnp.org/about-us/board-of-directors/

Although currently no tours are being led, please experience vicariously the wonderful Pua Po'o through the following description:

Pua Po'o, "Cock's Comb Cave," called sometimes "The Secret Cave" and sometimes "The Wild Cave," is a pristine lava cave discovered just a few years ago when Park workers were putting in a pig fence. You won't find it on any Park maps because its location is kept a secret. In the past, one day a week, a ranger led twelve lucky people, and only twelve, through this very special ecological treasure, and it was free! That's all changed though, as things do.

To digress for an instant, ah, the Hawaiian language is so beautiful! *Pua* means flower, and *po'o* means chicken. So Pua Po'o is a way of saying the flower on the chicken head. Much more poetic than cock's comb, isn't it?

This is a five-mile round hike (allow 6 hours) through the rainforest, and before descending down a ladder into the cave, the guide will ask everyone on the tour to promise not to disclose its location. Everyone is required to wear helmets with headlamps and leather gloves, which are provided. Also it is a requirement to wear long pants and closed-toed shoes. Pack a snack, too. Water, also, of course.

As of now, the cost is $60. It's really worth it! For reservation information, current prices, and dates and times, here is the website: http://www.fhvnp.org/institute/wild-caves-exploration/ or call 808-985-7373. Make your reservation early—these tours fill up fast. Private tours are possible. Call the above number.

What's so special about this cave? It's pristine! the way Nahuku, Thurston lava tube, probably used to be before it was discovered. And it's gorgeous and magical! Golden and silver lava icicles and lava stalagmites by the tens of thousands hang from the ceiling; the walls have untold numbers of niches with natural altars which turn the whole cave into a glittering cathedral!

The walls of the cave are coated with beautiful, mottled, whitish-colored bacteria giving one the impression of strange prehistoric art; this bacterium is currently being researched as a cancer cure. It is as much for this reason as protection for the cave that the leather gloves are required. **It is strictly forbidden to touch the walls of the cave,** in order not to contaminate it.

The cave is entered through a "skylight." A skylight is made when a small section of a tube roof collapses. Hikers must climb down a 15-foot ladder into the tube, scramble over slippery, sharp rocks, and walk about 25 feet in a crouched position over uneven surfaces. One must scramble over rocks and boulders to navigate through the cave, and getting out of the tube again is a fairly rough, scrambling climb. It is not a suitable excursion for small children or the elderly.

Pua Po'o is named for a stalagmite curiously shaped like a rooster's crest—a fin-shaped piece of lava with a series of small horizontal spikes. There are several of these odd formations in the cave; scientists have yet to figure out how they were formed.

Those who lead this tour are very knowledgeable, and present a fascinating glimpse into one of the least known ecosystems in the world—the lava tube, with its blind spiders and blind crickets.

I've made this excursion a number of times (when it was still free!); it always filled me with awe. If you want to experience this magical place, again, **make your reservation early.**

*So sorry this has been closed since the 2018 eruption. It's such a thrill!

Sandalwood Trail and Kilauea Caldera Hike
'Iliahi Trail
A fave short great hike! (2.5 hours or as long as you want to make it!)
Moderately difficult.

Ask at the visitor center of Sandalwood trail is open. Since the eruption of 2018, the trails down into Kilauea Crater have been off-bounds, except for this one, which skirts the bottom of Kilauea's cliffs. This is a lovely trail through a sulphur steam-vent area, with spectacular caldera views; it descends through rainforest down into the crater, up again into rainforest and then leads along the old Crater Rim Road. It does pass through the Sulphur Banks, so if you have respiratory problems, small children, or if you are pregnant, it probably is not for you. It is moderately difficult.

This hike begins at the Park Center. Turn right when you come out of the door of the Center. Walk past the Center, cross the street on the same side, and take the paved sidewalk. You will see the Volcano Art Gallery a short distance away over on your right, and closer on your right you will see a large sculpture. Take a moment to look at it.

In 2004, Hawai'i Volcanoes National Park issued a call to artists for proposals to create a sculpture portraying the concept of "wahi kahu," or *sacred place*. "Ulumau Pohaku Pele," *Forever Growing, the Rock of Pele*, by Kona artist Kalewa Matsushita, is meant to remind visitors that Hawai'i Volcanoes National Park is a place of natural and scientific wonders, and also a place that is sacred to Native Hawaiians. The sculptor said he drew inspiration from a kupuna, a Hawaiian elder, who envisioned the sculpture in a dream.

Just a short distance further on the trail, toward your right, you will see the hula platform, Ka "Ulu o Laka (the inspiration of Laka, the hula goddess). Here is where traditional hula and chant is performed. If you look to your left, you will see why this spot was chosen; the view of Kilauea from here is superb. Behind the hula platform is a reconstruction of a traditional thatched *hale* (house) where the hula dancers gather before and after their performance. Go off trail and have a look.

I wouldn't mind living in a house like this, would you? Minimum upkeep. No dusting.

After you take a look, get back on the trail and descend down this lovely walkway bounded by a cliff on the right. This is the **Sulphur Banks Trail**.

As you come out of the shaded wooded area, the trail becomes a boardwalk and the view opens up expansively. Huge cliffs on the right mark the outer Kilauea Crater edge; there is a signboard at the bench that explains some of the geological characteristics of this area. It's quite fascinating, really. Ahead of you in the distance is the great Mauna Loa. I like to sit for a while at this bench and enjoy the panoramic view.

As the path continues along, you will know you are closer and closer to Sulphur Vents so may want to hold your breath at times. Look toward your right at the beautiful sulphur banks; you will see deposits of minerals on the rocks. The bright yellow is sulphur. There is a sign describing the formation of mineral deposits in this area.

Do not get off the trail. These vents are hot and you could be seriously burned.

The path continues to meander along through Sulphur Banks. **See my description above of Sulphur Banks, for further information on this area.**

At the end of this walkway, you will come to the highway. Cross it, and continue straight ahead until you reach a trail junction. The one we will take is the middle trail. It has a sign that reads **"Sandalwood Trail**," (*"Iliahi Trail"*).

There is another access to this trail just to the side of Volcano House, but I prefer this route.

You will descend down past a grotto of huge ferns that look like Boston ferns; they are not but they are closely related. If it's a cold day, you can stop at this grotto and get warm; there are steam vents here, which is why the ferns grow so luxuriantly. However, **do not climb down into them.** A short distance further, you will come to a superb overlook of Kilauea caldera. To your left, if in season (late summer and early fall), you may find some strawberry guavas. Sample them; they are considered invasive, but save some for me!

Keep descending. You may wonder where the sandalwood trees are. Unless you are an expert, you won't find them. There are not too many, but there are some very young ones right on the trail.

The story of the demise of the great sandalwood forests, which is part of the near demise of the Hawaiian people, is tragic. You might want to read about it or ask a ranger. Basically, greed for sandalwood on the part of the aristocracy, the ali'i, to satisfy their desire for newly acquired Western goods resulted in forced labor of the common people which led to starvation and ruin.

Half-way down to the caldera, you will come to a fork in the trail. There is a bench here, and this is a lovely place to rest for a few moments and listen to the forest birds.

When you are ready to move on, take the path that descends down. You will amble now through a Himalayan ginger forest. This ginger is invasive, one of the most invasive plants in the Park, but just the same, the blossom of this plant is incredibly otherworldly. It is called "kahili ginger" in Hawaiian, named for the great feathered kahili standards used by Hawaiian royalty. The blossoms are as large as 18 inches, and fantastically fragrant. Even though it's a terrible pest, this trail is wonderfully fragrant during ginger season, which is late summer through fall.

You will pass huge many-ton boulders carpeted with damp moss. Look up toward your left to see where they came from! Not a place to be during a major quake!

After a short climb up and then down again, you will descend all the way to the caldera.

At the end of the descent, take the path to the left. There will be a sign saying that the other path straight ahead is closed. That path goes toward the eruption. You don't want to take it anyway!

Almost immediately after turning left, you will enter the caldera. It is marked by *ahu*, stone cairns.

Look up to your left. If you look closely, you will see an overlook; that's where you will be later during this hike. Take your time along the lava trail and admire the scintillating, iridescent colors of the lava. I love the crunch, crunch, crunch sound as I walk along here.

To your right is Halema'uma'u. This is as close to Pele's home as you can legally get.

I like to go off trail a little to the left, climb up on one of the big boulders, bask in the sun, and admire the view. It's also a good spot in which to meditate.

The climb out of the caldera is, predictably, kind of steep. There are some great views of the caldera just after you begin to climb out. Be sure to turn and look back behind you a few times.

When you reach the junction of Crater Rim Trail, as you climb up, there is a bench. Again, this is a lovely place to sit and listen to birds. Then take the path to the left.

Keep hanging straight ahead, and you will eventually begin to climb again. When the trail gets a little steep, you will come to a landfall with some big boulders. This was a landfall that happened during an earthquake of the 1970's; several people camping in one of the Park campsites were killed by the tsunami triggered by this quake. (Things do happen!) There is a great view of Kilauea Iki caldera from here.

When you come to the next junction, pause at the iron railing on the right for the view. For some reason, this is a place that the birds love, and it is easy to spot them from below, flitting about from tree limb to tree limb, especially in the evening.

Take the path to the left, which begins to ascend; it is clearly marked. The other path goes to Kilauea Iki overlook on Crater Rim Road. In less than a half-mile, you will go across a paved road where the trail picks up again. In a short distance, you will come to the old Crater Rim Road. You will know it by the jungle plants growing through its potholes and earthquake cracks.

Walk along this road a short distance. When you see a part of the road curving left, take this to another great view of Kilauea Crater. This is the cliff you saw from the caldera. There are a couple of picnic tables here right on the edge of the Crater where you can sit and take it all in.

When you are ready to continue, just continue to walk along the road ahead and it will curve back to the old road again.. Amble along; it will take you back to the Park Center.

Hope you enjoyed this beautiful, multi-terrain walk!

The Enchanted Forest
My Favorite Long Day Hike!
(Pack a lunch!)

This is an approximately eight-mile loop that includes one of my favorite wooded areas, the **Enchanted Forest**. You won't find "Enchanted Forest" on any of the Park maps—that's what it is called by some of the locals. It's a section of Crater Rim Trail. Not many people hike it; in fact, I have rarely encountered anyone else in the Enchanted Forest.

Read the sections on Kilauea Iki, Devastation Trail, Pu'upua'i, and Nahuku, Thurston lava tube. This hike encompasses all these sights.

This hike is moderately difficult but does require some stamina. This is the hike I like to take my friends on. If you have five to six hours and want to do a hike you will remember, **a hike that pretty much has it all, this is the one.** You will traverse gentle rainforest, climb down into Kilauea Iki, climb out of Kilauea Iki, traverse Devastation Trail, get panoramic views of Mauna Loa and Mauna Kea, hike the Enchanted Forest, and explore Nahuku lava cave. Bring lunch or a snack, water, and a flashlight. Also, bring light rain gear. One never knows.

Begin at the Kilauea Iki lookout. (You can also begin at Thurston Lava Tube. If you are beginning at Thurston, you will see the trail beginning to descend down on the opposite side of the street from the lava tube.)

From Kilauea Iki over-look take the path toward Thurston Lava Tube (toward the left, clockwise, as you face the crater). Hike one-half mile toward Thurston but stay on the same side of the street, then turn right at the pedestrian crossing over to Thurston, and descend down into the crater. Do all the things that people do down in the Crater, as per my previous description, and then ascend back up on the far side. It's one spectacular mile across.

After you ascend the steep steps (did I say steep?) at the top of Kilauea Iki, take the first path upward **immediately to the left** (in the opposite direction from the bench you will see). If you pass the bench you are going in the wrong direction. There is a sign that says "Byron Ledge Trail 0.1. Sometimes this path is overgrown with grasses, so you may have to look closely, although the sign is obvious.

Walk a short distance, about a tenth of a mile, and turn **left** at the junction. You immediately will pass through a gate (please close it again behind you; it protects the forest from pigs, and by the way, it's permitted) and in about ten steps, if you look closely, you will see a sort of footpath to the right. Follow it just a few steps to the edge of Kilauea Caldera; this is a great view. There is a log you can sit on and admire Halema'uma'u. **Be careful not to fall in! It's right on the edge!**

Retrace the few steps to the trail and turn right, follow it until it forks to the **left**, and take the left path. (You can no longer go straight ahead; the Park has closed that portion of the trail, there is a sign that says "closed"). Note how the terrain changes; it becomes much dryer and is not as lush very quickly.

As you emerge out of the forest, you will see Pu'u Pua'i, the red cinder cone you saw down in the crater, on your left. Hike up and up the trail of the small red cinder hill, but stop at the top, which is Desolation Peak, and sit and admire the breathtaking view of Mauna Loa, Mauna Kea, and Kilauea Caldera. *If* it is a clear day!

At the top, take a leisurely stroll straight ahead through this area. You may see Nene, because this is one of their favorite feeding areas. This is an ecological regeneration area; as you can see by the bleached tree bones, it was devastated by the 1959 eruption of Kilauea Iki.

Though the red ground cover you see everywhere is lovely, it is an invasive weed, fireweed. Still lovely, though. Probably would make a beautiful hanging basket. You may also see blackberries; eat them. They too are invasive. Save the ohelo berries for the Nene, please, though you might sample one or two.

*This part is optional. When you get to the beginning of the parking lot, turn left and take the paved path up Devastation Trail to another Kilauea Iki overlook, one-half mile. You will be standing directly over Pu'apua'i, that red cinder cone that is so visible from different areas of the Park. There is a picnic table here and rarely does anyone use it, so this is a great place to have lunch and rest. You are now halfway!

After lunch, **retrace your path the half-mile t**o the parking lot. Don't grumble about retracing your steps. It's an easy path, and you'll see lots you didn't see the first time. If you look carefully, you may see a few tree molds just off the path.

*If you want to shorten this entire hike by a mile, you can forgo the amble in the preceding two paragraphs, and just continue from the parking lot.

At the parking lot again, head across it. You will be going opposite to the direction from which you earlier came, of course. Cross the road (Chain of Craters Road begins here) and walk along the road on the left side about one-tenth of a mile. **You will see a sign on the left that says "Crater Rim Trail." Take this trail; it leads into the Enchanted Forest.** (There is also a "Crater Rim Trail" sign on the right hand side of the road—you want to go left).

The Enchanted Forest is a two-mile hike up a very gradual slope, through a lovely hapu'u forest with many native plants, especially a large collection of various ferns. When I take people into this forest, I ask that we hike in silence. And you may want to be silent too.

Why silent? So that you may experience the rainforest in all of its mystery and magic. Creaking tree limbs, whispering and sighing breezes, chirping, trilling, rare songbirds, the gurgling of shy kalij fowls and the singing Om of swordtail crickets delight the ears. The giant tree ferns, many 30 feet tall, wave their delicate, feathery fronds in the breezes, touching you gently as if blessing you as you pass along the path beside them. Rare endemic plants surround you at every turn in the trail— stag horn ferns, wild orchids... thimbleberry and wild strawberry abound.

This is the gentle woodland garden realm of Laka, the beautiful goddess of the forest. Nature spirits are alive and well here! Walk in silence and awe through a forest that once only bird catchers and sacred herb gatherers walked in solitude, and if you are attuned, you may feel how the ancients must have felt walking through this sacred ground—respectful, appreciative, and with tenderness. And maybe a little bit apprehensive. Take your time to enjoy and drink in the magic and mystery of this entrancing forest.

At the end of the forest trail, you will see a sign, "Crater Rim Trail." **Turn left,** and begin the walk up this wide, old trail way. It is now called Escape Road, but same say it was a path used by the ancients for centuries. Others say the Escape Road was originally built in the 1800's to transport tourists and provisions to the crater from boats on the coast. I like to think that it was an ancient path. Now the Escape Road serves as an alternate way out of the Kilauea Crater area in case the Chain of Craters Road gets blocked by new lava flows. Bikes and horses are allowed on this road.

At the top of Escape Road, after about a half-mile hike, open the gate and in a few steps you will arrive at your last stop, Nahuku Crater, Thurston, with its 1500-foot long lava tube cave.

The first section of the 600 feet cave is artificially lit, but the last portion, with its eerie dark entrance, looks foreboding. This portion is now closed, due to the ceiling falling. See the above section on Nahuku for more info.

After exploring Nahuku, cross the street, turn right and it's one-half mile back to our starting point, Kilauea Iki overlook. (Unless you parked at Thurston to begin the hike. In which case, you're home!)

A truly magical, mystical tour through eons of evolutionary time!

Escape Road From Volcano Village

Just across the road from the southern most entrance from Highway 11 into Volcano Village (where Volcano School is), there is a gate into the Park. You may see some cars parked here. Technically, you are still required to have a Park card to enter the gate, but it is unmanned and you are on the honor system. This is called Escape Road. This can be the prelude to a short amble or a longer trek from the Village. Bicycles and horses are also allowed here, but no dogs. Be sure and close the gate behind you to keep out pigs.

Escape Road was built in the 1800's to transport tourists and provisions to the crater from boats on the coast. I'm not certain but I have always felt it was part of the ancient trail system through the volcano area. Now it serves as an alternate way out of the Kilauea Crater area in case the Chain of Craters Road gets blocked by new lava flows.

After passing through the gate, by walking along the path a short distance, maybe a sixth of a mile, **you will come to a fork. The left fork goes to Thurston Lava tube, less than a half-mile hike.** At Thurston, if you continue past the sign to the lava tube, in a short distance you will see a gate. If you pass through this gate, you can continue on all the way to Mauna Ulu. (Please secure the gate behind you). Just be aware that it is downhill all the way to Mauna Ulu, so you know what that means!

If instead of the left fork, you take the right, you will come to Crater Rim Road East, the main Park road, in about a third of a mile. If you go anywhere from here, you will be on the paved road.

This portion of Escape Road is a nice place for a relaxed morning or evening amble—a hit of the forest to do one a bit of good. Take your time and appreciate all the tiny mosses and ferns, the textures, the colors, the sounds of the forest. A good path to amble with children.

Great Places Outside the Gated Park Gates
(but still in the Park)…

Lava Tree Molds
(Two for one! You can visit Bird Park just after!)

To get to Lava Tree Molds, take Highway 11 approximately 2.5 miles west from the Park entrance, toward Kona, to **Mauna Loa Road**, which will be on the *mauka* (mountain side) side of the road.   After a half mile, turn right on Tree Molds road to Lava Tree Molds loop. You can walk the loop road or drive it.   This short excursion just takes minutes and is well worth the time. Of course you can spend longer too!

Here you will see tree molds that formed when pahoehoe lava (the smooth, ropey lava) poured through the deep tropical forest.   The trees were too wet to burn, resisting bursting into flames just long enough for the lava to cool around the trunks. (Seems unlikely to me, but I've been assured that's how it happened.)   When the trees rotted, unusual deep pit molds were left behind for our enjoyment.

Koa and 'ohi'a trees surround the area in abundance and there are rails protecting the most prominent tree molds. The Tree molds range from 11 feet deep to 25 feet deep.

There is a difference between what are called lava trees and lava tree molds. *Lava trees* form when still-fluid lava flows away, leaving a freestanding shell composed of lava that solidifies in contact with a tree. *Lava tree molds* form when lava solidifies in place around a tree.

Peer inside the molds, and look at the interesting impressions the trees left. Another form of Madam Pele's art!

P. S. No restrooms!

Kipuka Puaulu
Bird Park
An easy, level 1.2 mile ramble

Bird Park is also outside of the gated entrance, approx. 2.5 miles from the Park entrance toward Kona on the highway. **It is adjacent to Tree Molds.** You can visit both at the same time. Turn *mauka* (toward the mountain) on Mauna Loa Road to the parking area for **Kipuka Puaulu**, as for Tree Molds.

Kipuka means an island of old growth surrounded (spared) by lava flows. *Pua* means flower. *Ulu* means growing. (Remember, Mauna Ulu? *Growing mountain*.) Hence, an oasis of growing plants. And underneath it all is a lava flow at least 8,600 years old!

The trail heads left and forms a 1.2 mile loop that leads to and from a giant koa tree, which is more than 100 years old.

Kipuka Puaulu has more native tree species per acre than any other forest in Hawai'i! The kipuka itself has more than ten feet of good, rich soil.

A kipuka, an area of land spared by lava flows, because of its isolation may become in time an evolutionarily unique bio-system. You may not see as many birds as you happen to hear, but you will definitely hear many birds. Besides the native birds, you may see exotic birds (in this case, exotic means birds other than our native birds), such as the house finch, northern cardinal, Japanese white-eye, kalij pheasant, melodious laughing-thrush, and red-billed leiothrix.

You will notice the difference in the size of the trees within the kipuka compared to the trees outside of it. The 'ohi'a outside the kipuka are young and small, but within the kipuka, the soil is old and deep, and the trees are much older. Koa and 'ohi'a thrive, along with soapberry trees.

This is a peaceful place to have a picnic, and there are tables here. Eat your lunch in this wonderfully fragrant forest amid rare birds singing their hearts out. Kipuka Puaulu is one of the few places easily accessible to the public where you still stand a chance of seeing either of the two living native butterflies, the Kamehameha and the Koa butterfly. Here dwell native insects and spiders in abundance. According to the Park sources, it has one of the highest diversity of native insect species in the Park.

You'll also find native plants typical of the mesic forest growing here, as Bird Park is now a protected area. It also is a collection of some of the rarest trees on Earth, including *Ochrosea haleakalae*, Hawaiin holei, a species of plant in the Plumeria family, endemic to Hawaii, *Sapindus saponaria*, Hawaiian Manele, and the giant koa.

We are so fortunate to have this kipuka—it was nearly lost in the 1700's when cattle and goats were let loose to graze. Because native Hawaiian plants have evolved no defenses to protect themselves, only tall trees were safe from being devoured. However, cattle were removed in 1928 and goats and pigs were fenced out in 1968.

The dieback of the 'ohi'a trees here is a natural phenomenon in Hawaii, but the ones here are dying due to old age and drought. According to botanists, it is believed that the dieback here and on the rest of the lower slopes of Mauna Loa may be due to frequency of El Nino droughts Hawaii has experienced for a few decades.

The Park furnishes a very interesting trail guide with much detail and many details if you ask for it. You can also view it online here:
https://www.nps.gov/havo/planyourvisit/upload/Kipuk apuaulu_Trail_Guide.pdf

Mauna Loa Road
(The Strip)

The Mauna Loa Strip Road, called locally "the Strip," connects the main part of Hawai'i Volcanoes National Park at the summit of Kilauea with the upper elevations of Mauna Loa. **If you have found Tree Molds and Bird Park, you have found Mauna Loa Road.** You can drive (if it is open; sometimes it is not) toward the summit of Mauna Loa on the Mauna Loa Strip Road for spectacular views at the road's end. Occasionally the Strip is closed due to fire hazard. There will be a sign if this is the case.

The narrow one-lane pot-holed road climbs and winds from 4000 to the 6700 feet elevation, approximately ten miles, and above that Mauna Loa Trail continues to Red Hill cabin on the East rift zone, and then to the summit of Mauna Loa. The Trail is for experienced mountaineers only. At the end of the 6700 climb, there is the epic Mauna Loa Lookout. On a clear day, you can see the ocean, Kilauea volcano and distinctive old lava flows.

In the past, the Strip was used for cattle and horse pasture and infested with feral goats and sheep. It is still degraded environment, infested with pasture grasses and weeds, but it is also home for many rare native plants and animals.

You will see koa, mamane and 'ohi'a trees, and many endemic bird species. In recent years, the Park has been restoring the Strip's habitats.

The last kipuka is at the end of Strip Road. Beyond is increasingly sparse scrub forest and lava fields. The Mauna Loa Summit Trail begins at the end of the road. There is also a short trail to view the endangered silversword.

All the common native forest birds are found in the area. **If you are a bird watcher, you must hike up the**

Strip. Walking along the Strip in the evening, with the sometimes magnificent view of the sea, is very rewarding.

Local cyclists like to struggle up this road, and then feel as if they are flying on the way down. This is a good place to walk a dog also, but keep them leashed, please. Nenes live here.

This is a great place to sit and watch the clouds roll over the ocean, if it is clear enough.

Want a real challenge?

Climb the 13, 678 foot Mauna Loa!

We're talking high altitude and a rough, jagged trail over risky lava in many places.

You can access it from two trail heads: Mauna Loa Lookout and Mauna Loa Observatory Road.

You must register with the Park, have adequate equipment, and training in high altitude trekking. If this is your thing, you can get more info and register here: https://www.nps.gov/havo/planyourvisit/hike_bc.htm

For an engaging account of a trek to the top, see here: https://www.nps.gov/havo/planyourvisit/hike_journal_vill averde.htm

P. S. Shhh. Don't tell anybody, but in July there are marvelous wild blackberries on the sides of the road to be had for the pickin!

Namakanipaio

How lovely! Namakanipaio means "the conflicting winds," and this is an appropriate name for this very lovely oasis of a camp-and-picnic ground, with its stately and fragrant groves of giant eucalyptus trees, for it often is windy, though usually pleasantly so.

Namakanipaio is located 31.5 miles south of Hilo. From the Park gate, it is approximately three miles south toward Hilo, a bit beyond Mauna Loa Road and Kipuka Puaulu.

This is a jewel of a place. I don't know who planted the now-giant eucalyptus trees, but I am forever grateful. I love to picnic here, a quick drive from Volcano Village, and it is so wonderful to lie in the soft grass, listen to the sound of rare birds and the wind in the leaves, and just imbibe the healing scent of the eucalyptus. It is at 4000 feet, the very crest of Kilauea, so if you do camp, please know that it can be damp and chilly, so plan accordingly.

This is a great place to bring children too. There are short trails to climb and open expanses to play in.

Namakani has a feeling of safety and serenity. Do try to experience it, even if you just drive in with your windows down to breath in the aromatic fragrance for a few moments. There is also a pavilion so you can picnic under shelter in the case of rain.

Namakani is no longer operated by the Park but by Volcano House.

To stay you have three great options, that is if you like the rugged life: You can stay in one of the 10 recently refurbished cabins. They are 200 square feet and sleep 4. You get a full bed and a set of bunkers with mattresses, linen and towels, electric lights and one electric outlet. You also get an outside fire-pit and grill. You don't get running water or a private bath, but the community bath has hot showers. Soap and toilet paper are provided. Cooking is not permitted inside the cabins. The fee is $80. per night.

The second option is to rent a tent and camping gear from the Volcano House, which sets it all up and takes it all down for you! You get a tent, an 8 inch memory foam mattress, linens, a cooler, a lantern, and 2 camping chairs. You can expand this to 4 people with another tent. There is a 7 day maximum visit. You also can use the community bath; soap and toilet paper provided. The fee is $15 for the site rental and $40 per night for each tent.

The third option is for those who have their own tent and gear. There are 16 campsites. The community restroom is available but not the showers. The fee is $15.00 per night with a 7 night stay. Fire pits and grills are available. First come first serve. Just grab your site, and put your money, cash or check in the box, the old fashioned way. For credit card payment, go to the Volcano House.

For all three options, collecting fallen or dead wood is permitted within 100 yards of the campground. Wood bundles are also for sale. Occasionally there is a fire ban. Cooking is not permitted inside cabins. No pets or smoking permitted.

Check-in at the Volcano House Hotel Front Desk begins at 3:00 PM and check out is at noon. All guests must still pay the Parks entrance fee, which is of course valid for 7 days. Please note: dogs are not allowed.

It is usually cool, and often damp, so be prepared.

Call **Volcano House at 1-844-569-8849** for reservations and information. Or go to:
http://www.hawaiivolcanohouse.com

Park information concerning Namakanipaio is here:
Nāmakanipaio - Hawai'i Volcanoes National Park (U.S. National Park Service) (nps.gov)

Keonehelelei
The Falling Sands
(Ka'u Desert Footprints)

An easy hike begins at the desert trail head eight miles south of the Park entrance on Highway 11, between mile markers 37 and 38. The entrance is clearly marked; there's an emergency phone there. The trail is less than two-miles round trip. Follow the part-sand, part-gravel path southeast away from the parking area; it isn't hard to follow.

Footprints fossilized in the Ka'u Desert ash hold a mystery, and no one really knows the answer, but there is a fascinating story around them that preserves an important event in ancient Hawaiian history.

There are two footprint-bearing ash layers in the desert, each separated by 90 cm of dune sand. The footprints can be found heading in both a northeasterly and southwesterly direction.

They were discovered in 1919 by accident. Who made these bare footprints, and when? How is it they are preserved?

The story is that they were made in 1790 by a group of warriors and their families, led by Keoua, the enemy of Kamehameha, as they made their way back to their home in the district of Ka'u, after an indecisive battle for the sovereignty of the island. The weary group camped on Kilauea at a sacred heiau (temple) to Pele, and then split up into three groups for the march across the desert.

The first party made it safely across. But as the second party was midway across, Kilauea erupted, volcanic ash and hot gas exploded from the caldera, and a thick cloud of ash, sand and rocks was ejected out of the crater and rained down for miles around. They were in the wrong place at the wrong time.

When the third party, not in the path of the ash cloud, finally gathered themselves together and marched onward, they saw ahead of them their people lying upon the ground, apparently resting. As they drew closer however, they realized that they were all dead.

The story tells how husbands and wives and children lay entwined together, their noses touching, which is the way the ancients communicated their love. Only one pig escaped death. Estimates of the number of fatalities range from about 80 to 5,405. A pretty broad range! The year was said to be 1790.

Hawaii volcanologists who have examined the mystery tell that most likely rather than a dense ash cloud, the unlucky warriors and their families were killed by a "pyroclastic surge," a stream of hurricane force winds, composed of hot steam and sulphuric gases.

This event had *huge* consequences for Hawaiian history. Keoua interpreted this tragic event as a sign that Goddess Pele had abandoned him, and soon after, surrendering himself hopelessly to his fate, he became the first human sacrifice at the great war heiau built by Kamehameha.

Recently archaeologists have found evidence that there were temporary dwellings here in this very arid place, which says a lot for the physical stamina and resourcefulness of the ancient people. After all, what did they do for water?

Archaeologists believe that they came here to chip away at the lava rock, collecting fragments for their tools. Some archaeologists have theorized that many of the footprints in the desert, rather than being the footprints of the ill-fated warriors, are the footprints of these people, mostly women and children for some reason, which would account for their small size.

You will reach a pavilion that protects some of these footprints. Unfortunately, they are weathered and have been vandalized. However, further out into the desert, sometimes covered by shifting sands, sometimes not, are thousands of well-preserved footprints.

If the tragic story of Keonehelelei, "the falling sands," captivates your imagination, you might want to do some exploring further into the desert from the pavilion. There are some beautiful rolling sand dunes with great vistas in every direction. Sunset, sitting on the dunes facing Mauna Loa, can be incredible, especially during full moon. There's an unspoiled loneliness about this place. My friends and I sometimes trudge in with our guitars and ukuleles, find a comfortable hollow in the dunes, and chant to the Great Spirit. It's that kind of place.

However, I would suggest you have a GPS receiver or get a guide. The Park sometimes has tours—check with the Visitor Center. If you have a very good sense of direction, it's doable during the day. But you could easily lose your way back at night. **There are no trails through sand dunes.** If you do get lost, always head up toward the mountain, duh!

There are many more footprints hidden in these dunes, some say thousands, and they are much better preserved; I have discovered some of these and it is thrilling to follow them a distance and imagine whose they were, and where they were going. The shifting sands of the desert, however, alternately cover these over and expose them again; once seen, they may never be seen again. Be sure to take plenty of water if you go exploring; it can get quite hot out here.

Pu'u Maka'ala and 'Ola'a Forest
(Unattended by rangers. Extreme caution! Hike into
this forest only with a guide)

**Pu'u Maka'ala (Stay-Alert Hill) Natural Area
Reserve**, named for a cinder cone rising over 200 feet, is
part of the much larger **'Ola'a Forest Reserve**. 'Ola'a
Forest is not contiguous with the rest of Hawai'i
Volcanoes National Park. It is composed of two adjacent
tracts of land separated by Wright Road in Volcano
Village.

Natural Area Reserves (NAR) are designated and
managed to protect unique natural and cultural resources
for current and future generations. The Natural Area
Reserves Program on the island of Hawai'i manages eight
reserves encompassing nearly 95,000 acres. Pu'u Maka'ala
was first established in 1981. It is not within Hawaii
Volcanoes National Park, but is managed by the
Department of Land and Natural Resources, Division of
Forestry and Wildlife.

This area is usually **open to the public.** Be aware
however, **it is very possible to get thoroughly lost here**;
trails are not maintained, few people hike here, and the
forest is dense and provides few clues to direction or
location—everything begins to look alike once you are
deep within the dark forest. Lava tubes and cracks lace the
entire area, and falling in one could be deadly. Pig hunters
also may be in the area, and you might be mistaken for
dinner. Secondly, this is some of the most pristine native
forests in Hawaii, abundant with endemic plants and
animals. Coming in here with seeds of weeds on your
clothing or shoes could be fatal to many of these species,
not to mention the dire effects of trampling upon them.

**If you do come here, do not come alone!!! Best
would be to have a GPS or come with a guide. A cell
phone might work. Might not too!** Bring rain gear and

warm clothing for sure! And boots would be a plus. You're sure to get wet feet here.

The Reserve protects almost 19,000 acres of endemic alpine rainforest. Hiking in Pu'u Maka'ala is allowed for groups of ten persons or less. Please make sure your shoes are cleared of foreign seeds. Hunting is allowed. Motorized access, camping, and fires are not permitted. Please pack out all trash. There are no facilities at the trail head area.

The 'Ola'a Forest is a part of Hawaii Volcanoes National Park but is separated from the main area of the park. It is a 9,000 acre parcel of relatively undisturbed rain forest.

You will get to the 'Ola'a forest by Mauka toward the mountain) at Wright Road in Volcano Village and traveling along a two-lane road for 2 miles. You will recognize your arrival at the south-west corner of 'Ola'a forest when you arrive at the Park sign. Go 0.6 miles further to the left bend in the road. The left side of the road is an open pasture. There is a dense forest on the right through this extent. Park on the right, at the end of the forest just where it turns into pasture. You will see the wire fence that encloses "Ola'a near the road. You can see many native plants even just without crossing the fence into the forest. But if you do want to go into the forest, enter the fenced area without damaging the fence, walk to the left toward the corner of the fenced area a few yards away. Turn to the right along the fence line and go a few yards until you get to a trail that enters the forest. You only need to go along this trail a short distance (50 yards or so) to get an appreciation of the general characteristics of this rainforest area. Take a look here for really good information and photographs on the native plants: http://www.botany.hawaii.edu/faculty/bridges/bigisland/ol aa/olaa.htm

Formerly called La'a, this elfin-like forest was a legendary place for collecting bird feathers. It was established to protect some of the Big Island's most important wet native forest and unique geologic features and it is an important habitat for some of Hawaii's rarest birds, as well as rare plants—there are 21 rare plants and four rare birds living here.

Follow Wright Road in the Village *mauka*, toward the mountain, and then turn right on Amamau Road and follow it until you reach the cul-de-sac. Then park and walk the grassy trail one-fourth mile to the trail head. You will see a sign and steps to climb over the fence.

This enchanting land is protected by Kuka'ohi'a Laka, the guardian god of the 'ohi'a forests, Uakuahine, the goddess of the rains in 'Ola'a; and Kuilikaua, the god of the thick mists that envelop the forests. In olden times, travel through this land was accompanied by prayer and care, as it should be today. **Traditions tell us that many a careless traveler found themselves lost in a maze of overgrowth and dense mists because of disrespectful and careless actions.**

The name *'Ola'a* connotes sacredness and sanctity; the root of the name being *la'a*, which means "light." An ancient mele (chant) celebrating 'Ola'a sings:

> *The birds fly like flaming darts to the*
> *uplands of 'Ola'a,*
> *Where the mist and smoke darken*
> *the forest,*
> *Spread out by the breeze which lays out*
> *the blossoms,*
> *Man is like q flower, roving about…*
> *Something that is irreplaceable…*

The lands of the upper 'Ola'a region were remote even to the ancient Hawaiians. It was most frequently accessed by bird collectors (for feathers), canoe builders, and collectors of other unique items for which the region was famed.

These lands are classified as rainforest, with nearly 100 percent native plants. There are alien weeds at the edges of the forest, but once you are in the forest, 90 percent of the plants are endemic to Hawaii, and found nowhere else in the world. That's really remarkable! The forest is dominated by 20 to 30 foot-tall tree hapu'u ferns, the largest ferns on Earth. These massive ferns have fallen, and tangled trunks and dead fronds make hiking off of the trail nearly impossible. One of the loveliest times to hike here is in spring, when the hapu'u fiddlehead fronds are unfurling; they seem to me to be some kind of benevolent aliens.

One surprise here is the giant nai'o, the "bastard sandalwood." When the sandalwood trade began to collapse in the mid-1800's due to greedy over-harvesting on the part of the ali'i, the bastard sandalwood nai'o was sometimes fraudulently supplied instead—hence its name. There are also giant koa here.

'Apapane, 'Oma'o, 'Elepaio and I'iwi are the four rare birds that abound here. If you're really into identifying native plants and birds, this is THE best place to find them growing and flying wild in Hawaii. It will be worth your while to buy a bird and plant identification guide or download one from the Internet.

Again, do take caution in this forest! Locate a guide! People do get lost. Notify someone beforehand with your plans, even if it is the host of where you are staying.

Kahuku

The Kahuku Unit is currently open Thursday-Sunday from 8 a. m. to 4 p. m. and is closed Monday-Wednesday.

The Kahuku Unit of Hawai'i Volcanoes National Park is an hour's drive south of the Park's main entrance. It is the 116,000 acre section of the Park located in Ka'u near the 70.5 mile marker on Highway 11.

The Park's website says, "Located on the volatile shoulders of Mauna Loa, the Kahuku Ranch was once one of the biggest cattle ranches in Hawai'i, producing beef and hides for more than 150 years. The apparent tranquility of ranch-life, however, was punctuated by volcanic violence that continues to transform the land to this day." I guess this depends on perspective—from the cows' perspective, considering they were used for "beef and hides," things weren't so tranquil on the old ranch.

Park rangers are on hand for information on guided hikes and programs. A detailed map of Kahuku Unit with trails, bathrooms, picnic areas and more is here:

The Kahuku Unit - Hawai'i Volcanoes National Park (U.S. National Park Service) (nps.gov)

Located on the slopes of Mauna Loa, one can explore the volcano's 1868 lava flow, native forests and historic ranch lands by foot. Guided hikes and programs are available.

The **Palm Trail** is exceptional for seeing the land transitions from the 1868 flow to the re-vegetation and re-forestation of pioneer plants and soil. You can learn a lot about native plants and their place in Hawaiian culture, as well as the history of island ranching. This is a moderate hike of two miles and takes two hours.

You can also enjoy a **nine-mile round trip drive** with a gain of 1300 feet elevation. You will pass steep, open pasture land, fissures and channels and lava flows from the 1868 eruption. High clearance vehicles are recommended above the upper trail head for Palm Trail.

The **Pu'u o Lokuana Cinder Cone** is a 0.4 mile loop with an elevation change of 100 feet. There is a short, strenuous 130 foot climb to the cinder cone. Go up the trail to the left of the hill, and on the uphill side is the route to the top through the cinder quarry. Stay back from the edge but enjoy the expansive view of lower Ka'u.

The **Pu'u o Lokuana Trail** is a two-mile loop with a 100 feet elevation climb. A guide book is available at the top of the trail. You will hike past historic ranch roads to a pasture hidden by trees. Enjoy lava tree molds and then follow the old airstrip back to the main road.

The **Kamakapa'a Trail** is a half-mile loop of easy goin' through meadows to the top of a cinder cone, with a beautiful vista of Ka'u.

The **Pali o Ka'eo Trail** is 2.1 miles with an elevation change of 410 feet. Start at the lower trail-head and hike one mile up the road. At the upper trail-head, take the Pali o Ka'eo Trail through the meadows. You will enjoy the beautiful views all the way to Ka Lae, South Point.

Plan to spend some time at the Kahuku Unit. You will be happy you did!

Bicycling
My favorite way to go!

I'm an avid biker and if you see a lone wahine cycling in the Village, it's probably me! You'll know me by my neon orange tennis shoe laces!

Before a few years ago, it was a world class ride to loop the thirteen miles around Kilauea caldera on Crater Rim Drive, and I did it five times a week, but now that half of Crater Rim has dropped into the caldera, it's not possible. You can still bike the paved portions of Old Crater Rim Drive between Kilauea Military Camp and Kilauea Overlook, and in the opposite direction on Old Crater Rim Drive, passing Kilauea Iki, Thurston Lava Tube and down on to the intersection to Keanakāko'i Crater.

One word of caution! Few drivers pay attention to the speed limits, so be very mindful riding on the paved roads, particularly Old Crater Rim Drive.

For other possible bike routes, before I tell you about my favorite route, check out the Park website here: https://www.nps.gov/havo/planyourvisit/bike.htm.

The bike ride up Mauna Loa Strip Road is exceptional, but only if you are in good shape! It's straight up! But of course, easy goin' down! The 9.8 mile bike climb to the top has an average gradient of 5.3% and there is a total elevation gain of 2,748 ft, finishing at 6,668 ft. You can read about the grueling climb to the top here: https://www.climbbybike.com/climb/Mauna-Loa/13767. And here: Mauna Loa Lookout Road (pjammcycling.com)

Sure you want to go to the top? Of course, you can also ride up just as far as you wish, and come back down.

In the following section, I'll tell you about my fave all day ride excursion.

Day Bike, Hike, Sight!

Pack a light lunch, take sunglasses and water and maybe a cap, plus a rain poncho. I like to start out early in the morning, say 7-8 a. m.

Begin at Escape Road off Highway 11, across from Volcano Village near the Volcano School. **You will see a gate there** and usually a few parked cars. You can park there. There is a Park self-pay box inside the gate if you haven't paid for a pass. Also, please wipe your shoes to keep out invasives. Ride two minutes to the fork in the trail. Take the right fork and ride less than one-fourth mile through the forest to Crater Rim Drive. (We'll be coming back via that left fork.) You can't miss it. Turn left on Crater Rim Drive and ride along being careful of cars because they don't follow the speed limits!

First stop! **Kilauea Iki overlook**! Stop and have a gander at what Iki might be doing. Then continue on a half-mile past **Thurston Lava tube** (stop if you want and explore the lava tube if you haven't already, or, you can do it toward the end of this route) and then continue on down, down, down the winding road. (Particularly here you want to be mindful about cars. In the shadows of the trees, they may not see you.) In approximately two miles, turn right at the **Pu'upuai overlook** (first right), ride two minutes in and check out Iki from this vantage point. You will standing right over that giant cinder cone! Then go back to Crater Rim Road and continue on about a fourth mile until you reach stop sign at the **Devastation Trail parking lot at the intersection of Chain of Craters Road.** Go through the barricades and enjoy the one-half mile beautiful ride on out to the **Keanakāko'i** Crater and see what Pele is up to in Halema'uma'u. Then ride back up to Devastation Trail parking lot. **Turn right onto Chain of Craters Road.**

Oh how I love sailing down this road in the early morning with the breeze on my face! It's a spectacular four miles down to Mauna Ulu—the tendency is to go fast but...take time to stop and explore all the different craters. You can pull out this guide and read about each one. Vehicle traffic is very light so you can really enjoy yourself.

At Mauna Ulu, turn left. It's about an eighth mile to the parking area. You can leave your bike and take a hike up **Pu'u Huluhulu** (Shaggy Hill) and here eat your lunch with a magnificent view (unless, of course, it's raining. In that case, put on your rain gear and enjoy a misty shrouded volcanic experience, which is also great!).

Leaving the parking lot, you will see a road on your right—that is **Escape Road**. If you have a mountain bike, it's four mile straight up via Escape Road back to Thurston Lava Tube. Half-way up, about two miles, you will come to a gate—you can undo the chain and open it—it is meant to keep out pigs and not people, so you are OK to open it. In less than a mile you will see a sign for Crater Rim trail, but **continue straight up**. As long as you are going up, you're good!

At the top, there will be another gate. Same procedure. Open and close, please. Your are now at Thurston lava tube. There's good water in the water fountain here. If you haven't explored Thurston, you can do it now. Or, you can sit on the bench, rest, and watch the tourists having a good time!

From Thurston lava tube, walk past the tube, past the water fountain and restrooms up a small slope, and you will see the continuation of Escape Road. It's about a half-mile back to your starting point.

Of course, you can do the whole trip in the opposite direction too. You would begin by taking that left fork on Escape road, riding through the forest past Thurston, through the gate, and down the forest to Mauna Ulu. Then you can return on Chain of Craters Road and Crater Rim. I prefer the first route.

This route is for mountain bikes.

For **road bikes**, you can walk your bike through the forest from the beginning of Escape Road to Crater Rim Drive, follow the instructions above all the way to Mauna Ulu. You have two choices to return. You can come back exactly the way you came, being very mindful of traffic on Crater Rim (people coming back in droves from seeing the eruption!) The **safer alternative** is to take the same route back on Chain of Craters, but in about three-and-a-half miles, when you come to the sign on your right that says "Crater Rim Trail," you take that two miles up through the forest and connect with Escape Road. **The difference is you will walk your bike up.** I do it all the time and love it. After two miles, turn left at the top junction of the trail with the sign that says "Crater Rim Trail", walk your bike a quarter mile, and you will be at the gate—just beyond is Thurston. From here you will get back on Crater Rim Drive, turn right. Ride past Kilauea Iki and in a very short distance you will see the gate on the right which is the road back to where you started. Walk through the forest again until you come to the fork. Take a left.

Enjoy! I LOVE this day excursion! I know you will love it too. Plan for a nice dinner afterward and early to bed!

There also is a tour group which offers e-bike rentals for self guided tours and also guided bike tours. Information is below in the Volcano section as well but here it is: Advanced tour reservations are required. 808-934-9199 or toll free 1-888-934-9199. You can book online at www.bikevolcano.com.

And now...
Volcano Village

Ah! Lovely, storybook-pretty Volcano Village!

An old hamlet of winding, forested lanes and beguiling cottages right outside Hawai'i Volcanoes National Park. At nearly 4,000 feet, Volcano Village is much cooler and rainier than the coastal areas, so pack warm clothes and something waterproof.

Here you will find accommodations (there are roughly more than 300 bed and breakfasts, inns, and guesthouses), eateries, and some great shopping.

A perfect place to live! At least, that's what all of us who live here think.

Summer day temperatures average 75 degrees Fahrenheit and winter temperatures hover around 65 degrees. Perfect! Of course, with all the rain, over 150 inches per year, the temperature can drop, and often does, considerably lower at times. Most people here treasure their fireplaces. I treasure my electric blanket! Fog and mist roll in most afternoons and evenings; these are quintessential Volcano scenarios. Volcano Village is kind of like a cross between an alpine village and Scotland.

An abundance of flowers, ferns, and rare birds, peace and quiet, art and great people make this paradise.

Do you like hydrangeas? This is hydrangea heaven during spring and summer! Never will you have seen such huge blossoms! If you are here at this time, take a ride mauka (toward the mountain) up Wright Road, turn right on Aumaumau, and you will see a mass of the largest hydrangeas ever! You will also enjoy all the animals and birds and other beautiful flowers that line the quaint road. (Did you know Madonna *hates* hydrangeas? What's wrong with that girl?)

This is also probably the safest village in the world; you can walk the unlit streets and lanes at night without a care. In fact, just walking around is one of the enjoyments of this perfect village. The people are unusually friendly and welcome guests. Don't even worry about Kilauea erupting; since we're up slope of the crater, we're safer than most other areas of the Island. Five hundred years ago, this area was covered with extensive lava flows, but since then, the summit has reshaped itself and flows occur on the southern flank of the Kilauea, away from the Village.

Sound confident, don't I?

Of course there's always Mauna Loa, but that's another story!

A Little Bit of History of the Village

Of course, Goddess Pele was the most famous of early residents of Volcano, and it's best not to forget that! The native people did not live in Volcano—not only was it the sacred home of the formidable goddess, but the rainforest was not as amenable to farming and fishing as it was close to the sunny beach areas.

It's my habit to sit quietly with my kitty on the steps of my tiny house in the rainforest and enjoy the evening descend. One evening I had an epiphany! I could see the sky change colors because there was an opening in the forest in my driveway—but I realized that before clearings were made by people, there would have been no openings to the sky in the forest. And in the rainforest, everything looks the same—tangled masses of Hapu'u ferns, branches, moss hanging everywhere—in the rainforest, it's easy to become disoriented direction-wise. I remember one time when I briefly stepped off a trail I have walked hundreds of time and somehow, when I returned to the trail, I walked over it and kept going in the opposite

154

direction. It was ten minutes before I realized I was lost—and then another 15 minutes of quiet panic before I found the trail again. I was shocked that it was so easy to get lost! Just a few years ago, a young woman did the same thing in the Maui rainforest and was lost for days—only by a sheer miracle was she found alive. There's not that much to eat in the rainforest—there are birds, but the small birds here are very wary, mostly stay high in the upper story, and would be difficult to catch. (I myself am not into eating the birds.) There are a few berries, at the right time of the year. Even making a fire by the primitive method of rubbing sticks together would be very difficult—everything is wet. For the native Hawaiians, the Kilauea rainforest area was revered with awe and great respect—mostly it was the King's bird-catchers, who hunted the birds for their prized feathers, and then released them, who knew how to navigate through the formidable jungles. Being lost in the rainforest could be as unnerving as being lost at sea.

When the first missionary, William Ellis, made it to Kilauea Caldera, there were two dirt trails used by the native Hawaiians to navigate Kilauea. One was part of the trail which circled the entire island along the coast, the King's Trail; the other was a trail from Hilo to Kilauea Iki. By 1880, there was a hotel on the rim of the volcano, Volcano House. A new road was put in from where Akatsuka's Orchid Farm is now, a few miles below the Village, to Volcano House in 1888. In 1910 Martin Porter of the Hilo Trading Company was granted 200 acres in what was to become Volcano Village. In 1911, land adjacent to this was subdivided and bought by grant by several wealthy missionary families and a few Japanese families, which is now in the 'Ola'a Summer Lots subdivision.

By 1914, 35 Japanese families were farming the area, while some worked for Volcano House or for the wealthy missionary descendants. Some were koa loggers, who drove their logs in wagons down to Glenwood and then the logs were sent down to the wharf on the Hilo railroad. Others worked on the narrow-gauge railway that was to run between Hilo and Glenwood. In 1927, Porter subdivided his 200 acres, which were bought by 33 Japanese families and Tsunesako Honma. Of course a school was needed, and so the 576 square feet one-room school house was opened, and it served as a Japanese community center as well. Weddings, dances and Japanese films took place here. It still stands and is called, you guess it! "The Old Japanese Schoolhouse." It is now owned privately.

In 1941, although one-third of Hawaii's population was now Japanese, many of these folks were "detained," including the principal of the Japanese schoolhouse, Motoi Shiotani and his wife. The Kilauea Military Camp, which had functioned as an army recreation facility inside the Park, became an interment camp overnight. In 1942, all Japanese schools were ordered to liquidate their assets. In Volcano, the school house donated their assets to Cub Scout Troupe 8, and the property continued to be used for community functions.

In 1950, the school reopened, but by the 1970's attendance had dropped, so that that the building was leased and then sold to the Volcano Art Center in 1989. In 2009, the owner of the Holo Holo Inn Hostel, right next door, bought the property, with the intention of keeping it in it original condition. If you go walking in the Village, amble along Kalani Honua Road. (The school house is on private property, so please do not go on to the property itself). It's a small red building surrounded by Sugi trees and camellias. It's a great example of the traditional plantation architecture of Hawaii from the 1920's to the mid-1940's.

You will notice in the Village many Sugi trees. These immense trees, planted by the early Japanese families, grow as tall as 225 feet. Native to Japan, they are called Japanese red-cedar or Japanese Sugi pine. It is the national tree of Japan and is often planted around shrines and temples—it was also planted in Volcano as boundary markers. After big storms, their needles and branches litter the streets, and the fragrance of pine is lovely.

For an interesting read on early Volcano, get Garrett Hongo's book, called *Volcano: a Memoir of Hawai'i*. Hongo, born in 1951, a poet and professor of creative writing on the mainland, returned to his Volcano family home to reconnect with his family roots. His Japanese family had owned the Kilauea General Store. He revisits Volcano, and his impressions of this mystical, magical place make interesting reading.

Volcano and Volcano Village are not really synonymous, although the terms are often used that way by island residents. Volcano refers to a portion of Puna, with subdivisions such as Fern Forest, Manua Kea Estates, etc. while Volcano Village refers to the actual village of Volcano.

Just for orientation, the main street of Volcano Village is Old Volcano Road, with two secondary main side streets which branch off it, Wright Road, toward the Hilo end of the Village, and Haunani Road, by the post office. All businesses and our post office are located on Old Volcano road, our "Main Street." Just for fun, I'll call it Main Street.

Things to Do in the Village,

Volcano Village seems to be a sleepy little place, but behind the scenes, things may be bustling. Some of the best artists in Hawaii live here, and they are always getting reading for shows. Painters, sculptors, fabric artists, quilt makers, jewelers, woodworkers, musicians…you name the art, we have an expert.

On Main Street, you will find the post office, two general stores, a hardware store, a laundry, and eateries.

Pick up a free community newspaper, *Cooper Center's Volcano Community News*, in the upper general store (the one next to the post office). In it you will find art happenings, community news and many other events. And you can take a look at their bulletin board too.

One of the first things to do in the Village is visit the cultural center of our sweet village, the **Volcano Art Center Niaulani Campus**, which is an adjunct of The Volcano Art Center, (the main gallery is located in the Park) and includes its offices, a gallery and classrooms. It's located on the main drag just a block south of the post office. You can't miss it. It's open Monday through Friday—hours vary. You might want to drop in on one of their many world class workshops and programs. Creative writing, ceramics, glass work, painting—you name it—if it's an art form, it's likely to be offered some time. Volcano Art Center has been voted the number one gallery on the Big Island consistently by our island newspaper. You can visit their website at volcanoartcenter.org, or contact them at 1-808-967-8222. For workshop info, you can call or email: workshops@volcanartcenter.org. They also offer virtual classes such as lei making, hula traditions, and yoga, some of them free! Check out *Yoga with Emily*—she's a fantastic teacher! She offers both virtual and classes in real time open to our visitors!

Among other many activities and events, such as cultural demonstrations, hula performances, and Hawaiian cultural classes, **Niaulani offers a guided one-hour nature walk on Monday mornings 9:30-10:30 (it's free!)**, rain or shine (often rain!) through the restored protected Niaulani forest where you can learn all about the ecology of the rain forest, but you can also go any time on your own, including after hours. Amble through a pristine eight-acre rain forest with no alien pests just to see what the Garden of Eden was really like! Reservations are not required but appreciated for groups of five or more. For a small donation, you can request a custom rain forest tour—they ask that you book one week in advance. Want to help save the rain forest? The Center also offers a hands-on 3-hour forest restoration learning and stewardship program, Please book one month in advance for this.

Have some fun on their website with some free downloadable learning tools—the Niaulani Plant guide, a Niaulani Trail Companion, the Niaulani Ethnobotanical Treasure Hunt and the Niaulani Ethnobotanical Crossword puzzle. You'll find them on their website under "activities." You can also do some great on-line shopping on their website.

The Volcano Art Center became the steward of Niaulani when they secured a 65-year lease from the State of Hawaii in 1996. In the 1920's it was designated a Forest Reserve due to its old growth koa and 'ohi'a. Mostly utilizing volunteers, invasive plant and animal species were removed to return it to its earlier pre-invasive state. You will love visiting it—you can get the feel how you could actually walk barefoot through a forest without any dangers. Garden of Eden.

They also sponsor concerts, often with world-class musicians, lectures by Hawaiian elders and storytellers, hula and many other events. Check out their website, www.volcanoartcenter.org for all their wonderful events. They have a bulletin board too just outside the building where you can find out about upcoming events and classes.

If you like art and you happen to be here during the Thanksgiving weekend, lucky you! The Village is renowned for its **Volcano Village Artists Hui Art Walk**, a time when Village artists open up their studio homes and sell their wares for discounted prices. Some of their homes are something like out of Architectural Digest; just to visit, talk art, and see their pads is great fun. But you can also buy great art! Reserve your accommodations early. However, it's a popular event!

In the summertime, you can enjoy the *Experience Volcano Festival*. There are local musicians, hula, artists in action, agricultural and cultural tours, and even a tour of historic homes! In conjunction with the Festival, there is Volcano's 'Ohi'a Lehua run, held always on a Saturday with more than 200 runners. This festival is getting more and more popular, with as many as 2500 visitors. For the exact date each year, visit their website: www.experiencevolcano.com.

If you are interested in participating in the 'Ohi'a Lehua Half Marathon and the 5K, visit http://www.ohialehuahalf.com/.

The "upper store," the friendly and quaint **Volcano Store**, is a wonderful mom-and-pop country store, selling all kinds of paraphernalia, including flashlights and rain gear, as well as hot dogs, good coffee, and homemade Japanese food, such as a "scoop a' rice." They sell my book *Bones of Love, Stories of Old Hawaii* too; check it out! They also sell beautiful cut flowers and anthuriums. It's fun to look around. There's a bulletin board at the entrance, and as I said above, you can pick up our local news rag for free. Out front you can find free brochures for lots of island activities. The old building was once a dance hall—the local wahines used to sell dances to the military boys, a dollar a dance (and I've heard other things too) back in the old days.

The other general store, the "lower store," **Kilauea General Store,** one block down the street, has a great coffee bar and tasty locally made pastries. You'll probably want to get a photo of Kathleen Kam's beautiful mural covering the store front. The Tripp family bought Kilauea general in 1987, and they also own Kilauea Kreations and Lava Rock Cafe just behind the store. You can also buy firewood here. Their Liliko'i passion fruit butters and guava butters, mango butter and Hawaiian chili pepper jellies make great gifts—but be forewarned—you can't stop once you start a jar of the Liliko'i butter—it literally melts in your mouth! They are locally famed for their Big O pizzas! Pizzas are take out in the afternoon and evening only; you can order from 3-6 p. m. They also feature hearty sub sandwiches, available all day take out. Call 808-967-7555.

Both the Volcano Store and the Kilauea General sell spirits with a huge selection (you know the kind), and both have gas pumps. Surprise! Gas in Hawaii is sky high! So be prepared!

You may see a **sandwich board just in front of our quaint Volcano Village Post Office** (the cutest little post office in the U.S.) on Main Street. This is one of the ways we announce community events. You may, for example, see a sign for our **Fourth of July** Parade, a real hoot, as some would say. Half of everyone and their dog (literally) in Volcano are in the parade while the other half watches. Don't miss it if you are in town on the Fourth. It's followed by an arts-and-crafts fair, a great silent auction, music, and lots of food vendors at Cooper Center. It's like an old-fashioned, traditional Fourth.

Another event not to be missed, and also advertised by our post-office sandwich board, is **the Mongolian barbecue.** This is so popular we have it several times a year. It's all you can eat at the Cooper Community Center for just a few dollars. More about Cooper Center coming up soon!

There are a lot of cottage industries in the Village. All those artists have to have a way to earn a living! The Kilauea Store sells some of their products. They are usually right up front on the counter. I don't know if they still sell it, but if they do, buy a bottle of "Holly's Dressing." It's delicious.

We're lucky to have a hardware store here—the **True Value Hardware** store is behind the Thai Thai restaurant. It's open every day too, because Vulcanites are always industrious, what with the always rusting pipes and repairs one needs in a place where if you turn your back the jungle takes over. Need a pair of sunglasses or a bong? They have them! They also have some groceries and gift items. **In front of Thai Thai is a tourist info center**; you can get brochures here for various island activities. **There is also a laundry** in the complex of buildings, right behind Thai Thai. More about the great Thai Thai later.

A great place to shop is the wonderful little **Kilauea Kreations** shop, just behind Kilauea General Store and Lava Rock Cafe.   In fact, the three businesses are all owned by one local, enthusiastic family.   Kilauea Kreations has one of the greatest selections of Hawaiian fabrics on the Island; indeed, it's renowned for them; that's because a lot of quilters live in the Village, but also some of the best quilters in the world are Hawaiian. The owner, Kathy Tripp, says, "The quilt shop was driven by passion." They have some fine examples of quilts hanging on the walls, and a selection of fabulous batiks. You can find a good selection of local art and other products here also—they feature over 200 local artists. And it's very reasonably priced! The number is 967-8090. Store hours vary since the pandemic. Highly recommended! Not to be missed! Take a look at the pit-fired aumakua artifacts there too, made by yours truly. And also this is another place you can get that great book, ***Bones of Love***! Visit their website kilaueakreations.com.

Another place to pick up some nice gifts is at Birgitta Frazier's pottery studio, **Da Raku Barn**. It's on the corner of Wright Road and "Main." You will see her obvious sign. She's usually open. She sells wholesale too! Just park and holler!

Harrowhawk Studios is owned by talented painter and metalworker Patrick Daniel Sarsfield. It's right in the center of the Village and he's only open by appointment. His number is 985-9934. I haven't seen him around lately, so he may not be available.

While Volcano Art Center is the cultural heart of the Village, **Cooper Center** is the heartbeat. Directions to Cooper Center—just turn up right onto Wright Road off Main Street.

Our wonderful little **Cooper Center Park** is a great place to take a pack lunch or get something to go and sit at one of the tables and enjoy the ambiance of the sweetest little Village in the U.S. Unless it's raining of course! It's still the sweetest but also the wettest!

Cooper Center also features a "world class" skateboard rink. Wander on over and be amazed at some of our talented young skateboard masters.

If you are here on a Sunday, you really are in luck. **That's because it's THE day for the Village**. It's the day when everyone comes out of the woodwork for the **Volcano Village Farmer's Market**. Ta da!!! Don't miss it!

You will find everything from ready-made, homemade food—Hawaiian, Japanese, Chinese, Mexican, Thai, Filipino, vegetarian, vegan—to flowers, art, puppies and kittens, locally grown vegetables, locally grown coffee and Volcano teas, honey, herbs...you name it; you probably can find it. There are also several vendors selling homemade breads and pastries. The fresh bread vendors are the best!

At the **Cooper Center Thrift Store** you'll find great bargains, even treasures! and their bookstore where books are just fifty cents. Most everyone has Sunday breakfast here—feasting on pancakes, pastries, tamales...because... **the Market begins at six a.m. That's right! Six in the morning!** It only lasts until about ten, so get there early or it's slim pickens. Sometimes there are Hawaiian musicians and hula dancers and occasionally a beautiful little girl plays violin.

The Cooper Market is THE social event of the town. If there is anyone you are looking for, or information of any kind you seek, gossip or otherwise, this

is the place to go. We love our market. (I do all my produce shopping there, and only go to Hilo once a month!). They even accept EBT. Just follow the people Sunday morning. Early! Here's an enticing link to a youtube video of our wonderful community center and market:
https://www.youtube.com/watch?v=ONoVuLl9UO0

Can't get up that early? Then hop over to the **Cooper Center Thursday evening market.** It's a newer market, and so not quite as many vendors—the emphasis seems to be on food. And great food it is! It begins at 4 p. m and ends at 7. Go early if you want to eat; most of the food vendors sell out.

Speaking of Cooper Center. This is the place where community activities go on. You can find yoga, tai chi, Hawaiian Huna, elder activities...whatever! Look in our newspaper (again, you can get one at the Volcano Store) or check out the bulletin boards at Cooper Center. You can look on their website, i68345.wixsite.com. (If that link doesn't work, just google "Cooper Center Volcano Hawaii). The Thrift Store, touted as "the best little thrift store in Hawaii" is open Tuesday-Saturday from 8 a. m. to 11:30; you can often find some true treasures among the castoffs. You won't believe the prices! And the third Sunday of each month is half-off! And if you need high-speed Internet, you can sit in the arcade and surf away. There is also a playground for children, and as previously mentioned, the famous skateboard rink is located here. Aunty Pon's Thai food truck is here Tuesday-Saturday. More about her later.

Who doesn't enjoy a good old-fashioned **swap meet**?! Well, Cooper Center has one **each 2nd and 4th Saturday** of the month, 8 a .m. to 12:30. Cakes, coffee, toys, clothes, tools, antiques, jewelry, food, music, plants and fruit and vegetables are to be had for low, low prices! The thrift store and bookstore are also open. Check out my artist friend Heather Penfield's table—she makes beautiful and unique jewelry, some very elegant silver Naupaka earrings and pendants and some very one-of-a-kind pieces she will love to tell you about. She's a master of healing elixirs and salves—I HIGHLY recommend her Magnesium Body Butter—put it on the soles of your feet for the best sleep ever! She's a reiki master and a culinary nutrition instructor—a wealth of holistic information. Visit her website at Heatherpenfield.com or visit her on Etsy at Theorchidnymph.

The **Kamahalo Craft Fair** is held the Friday and Saturday after Thanksgiving, featuring many vendors selling home-grown and hand-made products. Don't miss it if you are here then. That's the same weekend that the art hui has it's studio sale, so it's a great weekend to visit Volcano, but get your stay reservations made well ahead of time. Vacation rentals book up.

About the **Mongolian Barbecue** twice or more times a year. It's a benefit for Cooper Center. You select your own fixings and they are cooked right there by the chef. Everything is priced by the ounce, and you can take out. There also is entertainment. The announcement is in the newsletter and also via the sandwich board at the Post Office.

Besides the swap meet the 2nd and 4th Saturdays, and an opportunity maybe to find that Hawaiian treasure, what's any community without a **Cinco de Mayo** Celebration? We have one here, as well as an **Oktoberfest** celebration. For dates and more events at Cooper Center, pick up a newsletter in the Volcano Store or you can go online here: http://www.thecoopercenter.org.

For lodging, among more than 300 vacation rentals, try the best deal in town, *imho*, Laukapu Forest Cottage, run by Kathryn Grout, an enchanting, idyllic hide-a-way. Her number is 895-1418. It's usually booked up though.

Otherwise, check in with http://www.airbnb.com/ or http://www.tripadvisor.com/

If you're traveling on a limited budget, we even have a **hostel**, the Holoholo Inn. The number is 808-967-8025 or 808-967-7950.

Feel like some **body work** while you're here? Suzanna Valerie, 808-896-5661, is a licensed massage therapist. For acupuncture, call Eve de Molin at 808-938-6341. Rebecca Gonzalez offers massage therapy—give her a call at 808-333-5913 or 808-640-7656. Anela Scott at Pueo Healing Massage also offers lomi lomi and hot stone massage—808-300-6591.

For reiki, call Sandra Toles at 541-261-9892 or Heather Penfield at 808-640-2383.

Kilauea Nails offers manicures, pedicures, eyebrow, etc. by appointment at 808-937-4833. Lisa keeps all the Volcano *wahines* looking good!

If you're in the **Church-going** mood, we have The Village Church, telephone 967-8191. Sunday service is at 10 a. m. and Wednesday evening 6:30 p. m. It's up Wright Road, 19-4276 Wright Road. There's also New Hope Christian Fellowship, telephone 967-7129. It's a few miles down the highway toward Hilo town. Sunday service at 8:30. There's also the Society of Friends, every Sunday at 2 p. m. but call to confirm—808-443-9202. The Baha'i Faith meets 6-7 p. m. on Tuesdays—808-443-9202 but call first.

Like to golf? One of the most unusual courses in the world is right up the road, **The Volcano Golf Course**. The often mist-shrouded course may remind you of playing in Scotland. Isn't that where golf began? Take the Mauna Loa Road just a half-mile from the Park entrance, south toward Kona. I read that it was the first golf course in Hawaii; true or not, I don't know, because there was once another golf course in the Village. The old club house still exists; it's on Maile and Anuhea Circle, and was where golfers bunked overnight.

The present golf course began with just three holes, one of them inside the Park. The fairways were cow pasture, and they featured an event called "the Tomato Can Tournament." The cups were made from tomato cans! The home sites began development in the 1940's on Bishop Estate leasehold land. Volcano Fairways Estates opened for sale in 2008—these were the best parcels along the 14th, 15th and 16th fairways.

The Volcano Golf Course is now open daily 7 a. m. to 5 p. m. Their website is www.volcanogc.com and their number is 808-319-4745. They currently don't have an eatery but do have quick snacks.

Just down the road from the golf course is the **Volcano Winery.** They make their wine from their own grapes!

Volcano Winery was originally started in 1986 by retired wine hobbyist Lynn Doc McKinney. He planted 20 Symphony grapevines which did well, so then he planted 14 acres. Using exotic fruits such as starfruit, lilikoi, papaya, jaboticaba and grape blends, as well as honey, he created original and distinctive Hawaiian wines. In 1993, the Volcano Winery opened its doors. It was sold in 1999 but continued to be a family run business. After a fire in 2000, many of the original vines were replaced with French-American hybrids, including vinifera varietal and Pinot noir. In 2006, "Infusion" debuted, a wine made from Macadamia Nut Honey and black tea, the tea grown right there at the Winery. Other signature wines you can try are their Symphony Mele, Volcano Red, Guava Wine, and Blush. **They offer free wine tasting!** Try the Mac Nut Honey wine. Not for connoisseurs perhaps but tasty in a local sort of way. Their number is 967-7479.

Volcano Garden Arts, on Main Street Hilo end, is a place you won't want to miss. It's a unique indoor-outdoor "environment" featuring quality Hawaiian art and crafts, and a vegetarian restaurant. More about the restaurant below. You can stroll through the beautiful gardens of the 1908 Hopper Estate and walk the "Secret Garden" trail, surrounded by art. Art classes, such as bonsai, are often offered as well. There's a delightful Tea garden—I won't spoil the surprise—but expect the Mad Hatter! And don't miss the bromeliad garden in the back. Volcano Garden Arts is also the home of the Volcano Writers Group. If you are lucky, you will meet the one and only Ira Ono, the creator of all this beauty. You can also shop online: www.volcanogardenarts.com. Open everyday 10-4 p. m.

Wanna bike instead of hike the volcano? Bike Volcano offers rentals and tours featuring electric bicycles. The shop is located behind the Kilauea General store and the Lava Rock cafe. You can take a guided tour or self-guided tour. Advanced tour reservations are required. 808-934-9199 or toll free 1-888-934-9199. You can also book online at www.bikevolcano.com.

Not in the Village, but just a short drive toward Hilo, you can visit Fahrenheit 2400, a hot glass studio and gift shop owned by Michael and Misato Mortara, well-known glass artists. It's open 10 a. m. to 4 p. m. Thursday-Monday.

Also just a few miles outside of the Village toward Hilo is the famous **Akatsuka Orchid Farm**—if you like flowers, especially orchids, don't miss this place. Their hours vary since the pandemic—give them a call at 808-967-8234 and find out when they are open. The farm began as a family operation in 1974, and they specialize in hybrid Cattleya orchids. You are allowed to photograph them to your heart's delight. You can also buy them and have them shipped.

If you should decide you want to put down roots here—because magic happens—Allan Kroll is a well-respected Realtor, as well as a notary public. His number is 967-7187. Another local Realtor is Ronald Rigg. His number is 961-5255.

Volcano Eateries

Ah! Places to eat! The most important thing of all! All of these eateries, with the exception of the Kilauea Military Camp and the restaurant within the Park, are conveniently located on our main drag, Old Volcano Road, our "Main Street."

If you don't mind dropping some dollars, **Kilauea Lodge** is the premier place to dine. Look for the yellow lodge on Main Street. It was built in 1938 as a YMCA camp, called Hale O Aloha, House of Aloha, and is a National and State Historical site. It was originally envisioned as a forest camp for boys and young men. Its Fireplace of Friendship is something you will for sure want to photograph. Harold Lucas of the YMCA and Thomas Jaggar, the famous volcanologist, wanted to build a lasting edifice to friendship, and solicited contributions from every club in the International Rotary and Lions Club networks for stones. (By the way, we still have a Rotary Club here and it's going strong.) One hundred clubs and individuals contributed, and it was dedicated in the presence of 400 people in 1938. In 1942, the property became a radio school for the U.S. but after the war, and the 1960 tsunami which destroyed the YMCA building in Hilo, leaders decided to sell the property to buy a new building in Hilo. Virginia and Bill Dicks bought the property and opened a lunch shop famous for it "mile-high-pie," It was sold again when Highway 11 was put in, and later sold again to the Jeyte's, who opened it as Kilauea Lodge and Restaurant in 1988. It was only recently sold again, so we shall see what the new owners plan to do with it.

It consists of 11 buildings on ten acres. It was built in what is called the Craftsman style, an anti-industrial trend that emerged in the late 19th century, and featured hand-finished details to showcase the beauty of craft-work.

Featuring continental cuisine, you will enjoy the ambiance of the big old fireplace, the art on the walls, the lovely decorated tables. Desserts are great! You might need reservations for dinner. The number is 967-7366. Dress is casual. But you can also dress up! You can go there right after a hike around the volcano or for that special anniversary dinner. They also serve a nice Christmas dinner and it's a place to dress up and go to for your New Year's celebration, if you are in Volcano at the time. Dinner is served every day of the week, 5-9 p. m. Go with a local and get a whopping 15 percent discount!

The Lodge also serves breakfast and lunch, Wednesday-Sunday, 9-2 p. m., and they have really great lunch specials. Try the grilled cheese sandwich with fries. It's so big, you will have half of it to take home for dinner. They also have a Pau Hana, drinks and pupus from 2-5 p. m. each day. They also offer a picnic lunch to go, for $36 for two. They also feature a small gift shop. Their website is www.kilauealodge.com. And of course, you can stay in one of their delightful rooms as well.

The **Lava Rock Cafe** is very popular with locals and tourists alike and they tout themselves as a mom-and- pop cafe. You'll find them on Main Street directly behind The Kilauea General Store. They are a family operation, inexpensive and also serve huge portions (seems that's what people expect here?) and have a very extensive menu. You have a kid who doesn't like Thai food? Want to eat local Hawaiian Style? This is the place! They serve breakfast and lunch. It's a cute and friendly place. You will want a pic of the mural by the same artist who did the front of the Kilauea General Store, Kathleen Kam. They also have wonderful homemade desserts. In fact, they excel in them! Try the pumpkin crunch. Note: be sure and try their Liliko'i salad dressing and their delicious Liliko'i cheesecake. They also offer Volcano wines and local beers. Their number is 967-8526. Reservations are not needed, unless you have a big party. Open every day except Mon, 11:30 to 8 p. m., Sundays 8 a. m. to 2 p. m. Sometimes they have live entertainment, featuring Hawaiian music.

Thai Thai Bistro and Bar (no, that's not a misprint; that's the name), you'll find it on Main Street, is my favorite for Thai food. In fact, it's the best Thai food I've ever had! It's a bit pricey; expect to pay about $18.00 for an entrée, but it's worth it if you can afford it. Every single thing on the menu is great, but I especially love the Massaman curry. My very fave is vegetable tempura, which is a Japanese dish—it's not on the menu, so you have to ask them for it. It's the best ever! Be sure and take care that you order the seasoning the way you like it; spicy hot is spicy hot here! I always order "moderately spicy." The number is 967-7969. You can order take-out but they don't take reservations. They have a great selection of dinner wines. They are open for lunch and dinner 4-8 p. m. daily except Wednesday and Thursday; they have lunch specials also. The beautiful Thai lady who owns this restaurant is the essence of Thai graciousness. Www.lavalodge.com to see the menu.

There is also a Thai wagon, **Tuk Tuk**, which parks at at the far end (toward Hilo) of Main Street most days except Sunday and Monday. It's immensely popular with locals and tourists. Look for the bright green wagon. You get a big bang for your dollar. You can call your order in at 747-3041, sometimes—because often they are so busy they can't answer. Best is just to go there. Hours seem to be 11-5p. m. Or until they run out, which is often.

There is also **Aunty Pon's Thai** truck parked at Cooper Center. What days and hours are a mystery! When you see it, it's there! Seems we like Thai food in Volcano. Three Thai eateries in one tiny village!

The **Ohelo Cafe**, a bit pricey, has steaks, fish, and that type of thing. They do have good wood-fired pizzas and an extensive drink menu. The number is (808) 339-7865. They are open for dinner daily except Tuesday and

Wednesday, 5-9 p. m. You can see their mouth-watering menu here: www.ohelocafe.com. It's popular and a bit noisy—not a place for a cozy dinner but good food.

The best deal as far as "big" eateries in the Village is the **Eagles Lighthouse Cafe**. Or maybe it ties with the Lava Rock! Hard to say! (You can ask them about the name—we don't have a lot of eagles or lighthouses in Hawaii). It's just around the corner from the upper general store, technically on Haunani. It has outdoor seating only, which is sometimes a bit drafty for our typically rainy days. Of course you can get it to go. The food is great, and again, *huge portions*. They serve their own homemade bread and homegrown veggies, and their sandwiches must be the biggest in the world. Two people easily fill up on one sandwich. The potato salad is the best I have had, anywhere! Ever tried breadfruit salad? Ask if they have it—it's seasonal. But oh so yummy! You will probably need to adjust your belt. They also have mouth-watering desserts—try the cheesecake.   The number is 985-8587. They close around five or so in the evening, but they are open early for breakfast. What time I don't know, but early.

Cafe Ono, located just before the Tuk Tuk truck at Volcano Garden Arts on Main Street, is open Thursday-Sunday from 11- 2 p. m. You can eat indoors or outdoors in the beautiful garden setting. Cafe Ono features vegan and gluten-free as well as vegetarian fare, and the portions are huge! You will want to sample the desserts, possibly for take-home. Great salads and soups with locally grown coffee and tea. 808-985-8979

For something different, head up Wright Road mauka (toward the mountain), and turn right on Amaumau Road to the **Lili House** farm, a private family farm featuring an up-country-style tea time in front of an outdoor fireplace (for the up-country chilly mists) and a petting zoo! Home-made bread and butter and jam and berry scones are waiting for you, with coffee and tea. It's a lovely family

173

and you'll experience some real aloha! And best off all, you'll get to hang out with goats, pigs, chickens, ducks, cows, bunnies—all who love to be petted. This is a great family excursion and you'll wish you could live just like this! You can make your reservation at thelilihousefarm.com. Or phone 808-640-6325.

Something new is **Rico's Taco Shop**. It's a pick-up your-tacos and take home, and is located at the Aloha Happy Ranch on Main Street. Drive up Main past Wright Road and look for it on your left, before Volcano Arts. If it's open, they put a sign out on the road. Ask them if you can hi to all the happy animals!

If you feel like eating in your lodging, you might try one of these home eateries and ask what their menu for the day is:

Hangry Yeti Food— 808-940-7409
Hopper's Street Food—Text 808-494-4787
Sumthing Diffrent—text them at 808-722-7660
Les Hershorn—808-896-4845

If you are the type who likes to prepare your own food, you can get fabulous fresh garden veggies from **McCalls Farm**, which is about a mile up Haunani, just off Main Street. They sell at the market on Sunday morning, but also on Wednesday afternoons at their farm from 2-5 p. m. You will seen their signs all along Haunani Road leading you to their farm—the signs are only put out just before 2 p. m. Call ahead and ask what is in season and they will fill up a bag for you and put your name on it so no waiting. Their blackberries and blueberries are to die for. 808-937-1056

Outside of the Village and inside of the Park, you can eat at Kilauea Military Camp. They have the Crater Rim Cafe, the 10-pin Grill, the Java Cafe, the Lava Lounge and the KMC General store.

The **Crater Rim Cafe** is open daily for breakfast and dinner. It's a casual setting and on select nights they offer an ala carte menu and offer weekend specials. They also offer themed special dinner on holidays such as Thanksgiving, Easter and St. Patrick's Day, etc.

The **10-Pin Grill** is the small cafe in—you guess it—the bowling alley. Open daily, they offer typical American fare such as burgers, pizza, sandwiches as well as beer.

The Lava Lounge offers drinks and cocktails, as well as live music on the weekends. A lot of Volcano locals frequent it on the weekends. Call 808-967-8365. They were open daily 4- 7 p. m. and 4-9 p. m. on Friday and Saturday. Be sure and have a designated driver.

The **KMC General Store** offers some food items, household items, curious, gifts toiletries and firewood.

You can also eat at the restaurant within the park, **The Rim at Volcano House**, right across from the park headquarters, while enjoying the fantastic view over Kilauea caldera. Go before sunset for the great view over the caldera. Astounding! Fairly pricey, but good food. They are open for breakfast, 7-10:30 a. m., lunch 11-2:30, and dinner 5-8 p. m. For reservations call 808-930-6910. They feature Hawaiian music at dinner. You can see the menu at www.hawaiivolcanohouse.com.

Uncle George's Lounge is right next to The Rim restaurant. You can get an afternoon snack or late night treat, wine, bear and cocktails. If you are staying at Volcano House, you can also get in room dining from 11 a. m. to 10 p. m. There are some cozy chairs in front of the lounge where you can sit and sip a drink, listen to the music, and enjoy the view of the caldera.

So you can see, we eat very well in our little village!

***

Well, that's about it, for now. Volcano Village is not the Big Apple or Paris, (thank goodness!!!) but it is the most magical place on Earth! In my humble opinion, of course. I wouldn't want to live anywhere else! Just take a stroll through the Village and see for yourself!

And lastly, check out:

http://www.VolcanoVillageHawaii.com/ for more great and updated information on Volcanoe Village and Hawai'i Volcanoes National Park.

I wish with all my heart you enjoy your visit to Kilauea volcano, and especially to Volcano Village. And if you see a wahine wearing tennis shoes with neon orange laces on the trail, on a bike, or walking through the Village, give me a shout!

Kilauea Eruption 2018!
Our last not-so-long-ago eruption!
What's it like to live through an extended volcanic eruption?

Up here in Volcano Village, less than three miles as the crow flies from the caldera of the world's most active volcano, there were 400-600 earthquakes a day during the surprise eruption of 2018! There were hundreds of quakes we could not feel at all, there were many that registered through our bodies as a kind of hum so subtle we weren't sure they were "real" or not, there were many in the three and four point magnitude range, and then there were the 5.2's.

Oh the 5.2's! They registered daily with an almost supernatural occurrence, at first approximately 24-28 hours apart. (Later they would occur further and further apart; surely the volcano has a life pulse of its own!) Our houses would shake, rattle and roll, my giant disco ball hanging from the ceiling (under which I do my yoga! and which turned out to be a great personal seismograph!) would swing violently between the rafters. I made a YouTube video of it during a 6.9 quake and set it to Beethoven's Fifth—you can see it here: https://www.youtube.com/shorts/-Z2tBV3QL68. Our roads would crack and yawn somewhere we never knew where, and we learned to expect that 20 miles down slope, the raging river of molten lava would, in an hour or so after the recurring 5.2, receive an impetus to spew forth violently an increase in the rate it was pumping the fiery molten lava and gasses out.

Within minutes of the daily 5.2, there would also be a belch of black smoke, composed of dust and rock and ash from the heart of Kilauea, Halema'uma'u Crater. This dark cloud carried poisonous gasses and particles of silica ash, basically tiny particles of glass, whose respiratory effects on plants, animals and humans we don't know too much about yet. But, it doesn't seem to be that good! And so we were issued gas masks and told not to go outdoors. Up here in one of the most rare and precious rainforests on planet Earth, we feared for the endangered birds and insects and beautiful and fragile rare plants and trees, as well as for ourselves and our pets. We couldn't drink our water, since all of us are on water catchment and depend on the rain, which had been contaminated with the ash fall. Sometimes we were on pins and needles wondering if and when we would get the call to evacuate, but more often we were strangely calm, peacefully resigned to whatever was going to happen.

The 5.2's were not technically earthquakes, but were called "collapse events." These collapse events, when portions of the existing caldera began to fall into the deep pit where the lava lake had once existed, created the force responsible for altering Kilauea caldera to the point where, 12 weeks later, it was unrecognizable when compared to what Kilauea caldera had looked like before. More about this later!

Whatever was *going* to happen, we knew we were in the midst of experiencing, whether we liked it or not, one of the great historical eruptions of Kilauea. We anxiously watched the reports from Hawaiian Volcano Observatory and USGS to try to understand the science of it all, so that we could make our own homespun predictions. Not that we didn't trust the scientists, but they freely admitted they didn't know what was going to happen either.! We became amateur volcanologists and geologists, searching for ever more dated and obscure science articles on previous eruptions of Kilauea. We became familiar with the language of the earth sciences, and its vocabulary glided off our tongues more and more glibly as we discussed this or that predictive theory. Our theories and predictions changed daily, as the eruption changed.

We were in completely uncharted territory. Where were the fountains of lava going to break out next? Was the giant river of lava going to change direction and spare or take our homes and our most beloved beaches and play spots? Was the wind going to change direction and blow the toxins into our homes and faces? Was the next quake going to be "the Big One"? Was a pyroclastic surge, a fluidized mass of turbulent gas and rock fragments that could travel at the rate of 300 miles per hour, like the one that killed every inhabitant but one in the city of Saint-Pierre in Martinique in 1902, imminent?

Should we evacuate? Where was it safe to go? Should we encourage visitors to come, and keep our island tourist industry alive, or should we tell them to go else where, we just couldn't guarantee their safety? Should we make sure our wills were in order and our final wishes known?

Every few hours we checked into Facebook or PunaWeb Forum or various videographers' blog sites to find out first hand from our fellow kamaaina's (locals) what was happening down at the flow, and what was happening up here on the summit. We heard whose home had been taken, whose home might be spared, and whose home was threatened next. Out of the 700 homes overtaken by the river of lava or burnt to the ground, ten of those were the homes and farms, the lifework of, the fortunes of, my friends. We all knew people who lost everything.

We saw on the news, which was usually available a day later than what we could find out via the cyber coconut wireless, summaries of what we already knew, but they were accompanied with attention grabbing-headlines that went round the world, and sometimes we laughed at them, they seemed so exaggerated. "Big Island Hawaii destroyed by monster volcano!" "Thousands Flee Hawaiian Fury!" But were they? Maybe we laughed out of nervousness? It seemed like a dream, to many a nightmare—could this be really happening to us? We saw magnificent photos and we watched the awe-inspiring videos via brave souls that dangled out of helicopters which flew through the smoke and haze of fire and risked plunging into the raging lava below, and those who jeopardized their lives documenting on foot their own neighborhoods that were "going up in smoke" so to speak.

We watched with sadness and compassion the people with little children and their pets who camped out in evacuation shelters. We watched on social media the numbers of people trying to evacuate their farm animals, or find their lost pets. We read Civil Defense warnings that popped up on our phones many times a day.

But behind this "true life" experience, the nitty-gritty facts of our changing island life through these volatile earth alterations which were completely beyond our control, many of us were having another kind of experience.

It was the one described poetically in old oral histories of the ancient Hawaiians and now preserved in writing. We had heard it before, chanted and danced to through the beautiful hula, or re-imagined by island artists. It was the mythic experience of a great fire goddess, the creator and destroyer of the earth, the birther and the burier, the goddess of lightening, wind, and the dance.

Her name is Pele. And we were having her experience.

She had become real to us.

Whereas before the events of 2018 the word Pele was an abstract association and cultural symbol of volcanic and geological events, now it was the name of something real that was happening to us; it was the name of a power, it was a force. It was the name of a force before which all other living beings are powerless. It was the name of something that caused us to come close to our mortality, our impermanence, the impermanence of our dreams, our homes, our financial security, our jobs, the fabric of our lives.

Pele was scary and threatening. But she was also beautiful and awesome. Though we ran from her as fast as we could when she was coming our way, we couldn't get enough of seeing her beauty, of hearing of her astounding feats.

She rampaged furiously through the land, burying everything in her path with 60 feet of molten lava, if she didn't burn it to the ground first. Where a home or farm once stood, now stood six story high layers of congealing, smoking and seething lava. She burst into steam at the sea's edge, destroying natural bays and pools with their teeming creatures of turtles and exotic fish as we wept for them, transforming places we loved into gleaming and barren black sand beaches. We had thought they were ours forever. We learned that nothing is forever, not even the contours of the Earth. She drove people and animals away with her toxic gasses, and she frightened them away with her hissing and thundering.

She was terrifying.

But sometimes, even in her fury, she seemed benevolent. Or maybe she was just being whimsical. She spared homes where all around every other house was taken. She spared the geothermal plant. Just to show she could. She came right to edge of one of the fave beach playgrounds, and stopped right at the boat dock! Just to show she could.

The Beginning

It all began (of course there is no real "beginning," but a continuity of earth events) April 17, 2018. The molten lava lake in Halema'ma'u Crater had been putting on a real show for months. The scene was surreal and dramatic. Especially at night, from the vantage point of Hawai'i Volcanoes Observatory, perched over Kilauea caldera exactly on the spot where once an ancient sacred heiau to Pele had once stood, where now thousands of tourists and locals viewed it every day, the lake sputtered and fountained like fireworks.

I had been going to the lava lake several nights a week to watch the show, the eerie glow highlighting the walls of the cliffs, the display of pyrotechnics with which Pele regaled us. The lake looked like a witch's brew in a cauldron. Little did we know what Pele was stirring up! Tourists, huddled against the wind and the cold, oohed and ahhed as the scene below changed minute by minute.

A little over a week later the lake was overflowing the edges of Halema'uma'u, a real treat for those of us mesmerized by Pele's ever-changing antics. It was very rare that the lake bubbled over onto the caldera floor. In the East Rift Zone, Pu'u O'o was erupting less volume, with small flows at the cone and in the crater.

On April 30, something remarkable happened, and scientists began to really sit up and pay attention. To understand, let me tell you a bit about Pu'u O'o.

Pu'u O'o, "the hill of of the digging stick," an appellation referring to Pele and her pastime of digging craters, a cinder/spatter volcanic cone on the East Rift Zone of Kilauea volcano that had been erupting continuously since January 1983, collapsed. Pu'u O'o had over the course of 35 years erupted 2.7 cubic kilometers (0.65 cu miles) of lava covering more than 117 square kilometers (45 square miles) creating 230 acres of new land on the southeast coast of the Big Island. The eruption had taken out 189 buildings (including a church, a store, the Waha'ula Visitor Center, many ancient archaeological sites and 14 kilometers (8.7) miles of highways. All had been buried under lava up to 115 feet high.

Beginning in a remote part of the rainforest on the East Rift Zone, the 1983 eruption localized at last at the Pu'u O'o vent, where Pele began building her latest cinder cone. She also built a long lava tube that allowed the channel of lava to flow a long distance. Then she began her mighty destruction, destroying the towns of Kalapana and Kaimu, and also beloved Black Sand Beaches. It was the beginning of her game of cat and mouse. She built ponds, lava tubes, vents, and then moved elsewhere; however, Pu'u O'o fed everything. It was now a cone 2290 feet tall (700 meters).

From the top of Mauna Ulu, one of my fave places within the Park to hike, on a clear day, one could see Pu'u O'o belching smoke off in the distance. From far away, it was a peaceful scene. The Mauna Ulu eruption itself, which occurred before O'o was formed, was the longest-lasting and most voluminous eruption of Kilauea in 2200 years. It erupted from May 24, 1969 to July 22, 1974, a total of 1774 days.

Mauna Ulu lava shield grew 400 feet (121 meters) tall. Lava flowed seven miles (12 km) to the sea, covering 40 square miles (95.5 square km) of land, and creating 150 acres of new land. It had belched out enough lava to pave a road to the moon! On July 19-22, 1974 the lava lake at its summit disappeared from view, and the eruption was declared over.

Nine years later, Pu'u O'o began erupting in January of 1983, and after it's initial shock and awe, Hawai'i residents settled into a more or less complacent acceptance of the long years of activity. It seemed an eternal part of the landscape, so when its crater floor suddenly dropped April 30, everyone suspected something extraordinary was happening.

The floor of Pu'u O'o Crater collapsed as subsurface pressure forced open a pathway for magma to travel from Pu'u O'o into the Lower East Rift Zone (LERZ). The pathway followed a well-established magma transport system within the volcano that last saw a magma intrusion in 1960. As magma moved out, pressure decreased in the summit's magmatic system and Halema'uma'u's lava lake level began to drop. The summit also began to deflate due to the pressure decrease, because magma stored beneath the summit began to drain into the LERZ.

As the summit subsided, earthquakes increased. Previously about 10 quakes a day averaged at the summit, but this would increase so that by late June, the average was 600 per day. What was causing them?

On May 1, USGS issued an alert that there was the likelihood of a Lower East Rift Zone eruption.

On May 2, to the amazement of residents, little cracks began to open in the LERZ in Leilani Estates, a community 23 miles from Hilo, and just three miles from the town of Pahoa, and about 22 miles from the summit, as the crow flies. That was all so far, no high temperatures or steam, just cracks. But, the lava lake at the summit began to drop.

I was out riding my bike on May 3 when there was a 5.0 quake. I happened to look up and see a huge, pinkish-orange cloud out in the distance, in the direction of Pu'u O'o. What was it? My neighbors came out and we watched and surmised what it could be.

It was a plume of ash. More of the floor of Pu'u O'o had collapsed. The extreme heat from the volcano had caused igneous rock in Pu'u O'o to oxidize and chemically react with oxygen, turning it red. It was beautiful.

Little did we know—the eruption had begun!

The cracks in Leilani estates began erupting lava. Residents were ordered to evacuate.

By the next day, May 4, there were six fissures erupting with spatter thrown 100 feet high (30m). At 12:32 pm, a magnitude 6.9 earthquake struck. That's the one I made a video of—with my giant disco ball swaying. It was the largest quake in Hawaii since 1975, and was felt all the way to Oahu. Another large ash plume at Pu'u O'o was emitted, and a 5.3 quake followed. The seismicity, the rate and magnitude of earthquakes at the summit began to escalate.

On May 5, two more fissures opened in Leilani Estates, and on May 6, the number had increased to 10. The first house was consumed by lava. The lake at Halema'uma'u dropped an incredible 220 meters below the crater rim. Scientists predicted a long eruption.

On May 7, one fissure became inactive, but two more erupted. The ground began to crack extensively, crossing Highway 130. The fissures were no longer erupting spatter, but were steaming and emitting gasses heavily.

On May 8, the fissures increased to 14. On May 9, the ground was continuing to crack, the summit lake continued to drop, another fissure opened, and USGS issued a warning: there was a strong possibility of a summit explosion. Twenty-seven homes had been destroyed. Pele intended to destroy everything in her path, and nothing could stop her.

Evacuation Centers opened in Pahoa and Keaau. Many people had left their homes with nothing but their pets, if they could retrieve them, and if they were the luckier ones, a few personal belongings. It all seemed like a dream, a bad dream.

On May 10, all the fissure eruptions paused. That was good news; however, the quakes and deformation continued. The lava lake at Halema'uma'u completely disappeared from sight at a depth of 1070 feet (325 meters).

Fissure 16 opened May 12 but died a few hours later. The next day, two new fissures opened. They popped up in people's backyards. Large bombs of molten lava two to three meters in diameter were thrown up 400 feet into the air. These bombs were lethal if one should get hit by one. The lake was still dropping, and the volcano was still deflating. Scientists predicted that when the lake subsided to the water table, a huge explosion could take place.

One day later, fissure 19 opened up. Fissure 17 was fountaining and its blasts could be heard for miles. The lake continue to drop and the summit continued to deflate.

On May 15, a huge rockfall within Halema'ma'u Crater sent an ash plume 12,000 feet (3660) into the sky. The aviation color code was increased to red alert. Several fissures in Leilani Estates which had become dormant reactivated, and a new fissure opened. The summit was still deflating and lake was still dropping. The next morning, a 4.2 earthquake caused an ash plume 8200 feet high. Ballistic blocks 60 cm large were emitted in the parking lot overlooking Kilauea Crater, and cracks on Highway 11, just outside of Volcano Village and the Park entrance, opened up. The people in the area felt a number of after shocks.

On May 17, a huge ash plume of 30,000 feet was emitted at the summit, caused by an explosive event which was as yet not understood. The people of Volcano Village and its environs were shocked. We had felt we were immune from any real danger; after all, as close as we were to the main caldera, we were *above* the caldera. A new fissure opened up below in Leilani, bringing the total to 22. The volcano continued to deflate and the lava lake continued to drop.

The next afternoon, a fast moving pahoehoe flow crossed Pohoiki Road, and a new fissure, number 23, opened. Spattering was occurring now from fissures 15, 17, 18, 20, 21, and 22. Lava flows were erupting from fissures 17, 18, and 20. Still the lake was dropping, and the summit was deflating. Things were intensifying.

My doctor and his artist wife lost their beautiful estate, including her studio and many outdoor sculptures. They had taken refuge in their office in Pahoa, but not believing their home was truly in danger, they had taken few personal belongings with them. They were to regret it.

On May 19, an explosion at the summit sent an ash cloud toward the south. Fissures 16-20 merged. USGS issued a warning to expect more quakes.

The merged fissures split into two rivers, and both made it to the ocean on May 20. The next day saw more explosions at the summit, with ash clouds as high as 7000 feet. Fissure 22 was very active. Civil Defense warned about laze danger, a mixture of lava and haze that was toxic.

For the next few days, explosions at the summit continued, the lava continued to flow southeast to the coast, and fountaining continued from a number of the fissures. On May 25, amid numerous earthquakes at the summit, a new subsidiary pit opened on the north part of the floor of Halema'uma'u Crater. Kilauea Caldera continued to subside, and rockfalls and explosions continued. Meanwhile, the flow in two channels was entering the ocean near MacKenzie State Park.

On May 26, an ash cloud 12,000 feet high was emitted from the summit, which continued to subside. The eruption below had now covered 2372 acres (3.7 square miles) of land. On May 27, fissure 24 opened up. Fissure 21 was feeding an 'a'a flow that was advancing right to the edge of the geothermal plant. Flammable liquid had been removed from the plant, but people were angry that the plant had been built so close to the volcano, raising fears that toxic gas could be released if lava damaged the wells.

On May 28, an explosion at the summit sent an ash cloud 10,000 feet into the air. Quakes continued as Kilauea continued to subside. Some fissures died but others, notably, in retrospect, Fissure 8, which I will capitalize out of respect, reactivated. By May 29, Fissure 8 was flowing vigorously, fountaining 200 feet into the air. Pele's hair began drifting downwind from Fissure 8. People were warned to keep their pets indoors, so that the long glassy filaments would not be embedded in their paws and eyes and ears.

By June 3, as other fissures became inactive, Fissure 8 became increasing vigorous. Pele's hair was accumulating in Leilani Estates. Earthquakes increased to more than 500 per day at the summit and ash clouds continued at the summit; the summit continued to subside. On June 4, the flow front was 500 yards wide, and had built a delta extending 700 yards into Kapoho bay. The walls of Halema'uma'u were collapsing amid the numerous quakes. Scientists realized that these were not actual quakes from the movement of faults, but instead were caused by the impact of collapsing walls and rockfalls as Kilauea caldera and Halema'uma'u subsided. They began to call them "explosive events" rather than quakes. For us up here in the Village, it didn't matter what you called them...a rose by any other name...

USGS offered two possibilities about Halema'uma'u vent...it could be pau, finished, and would no longer be an active lava vent and would just be a steam vent, or it could be filled with a massive amount of rock and would eventually fill back up with lava...which would take a long time. Of course, Halema'uma'u has been the very heart of Kilauea for centuries, so it was difficult to imagine it becoming dormant. Was it possible that Fissure 8 might become the new heart of Kilauea?

On June 5, a curious pattern was to commence. It began with an explosion at the summit followed or concomitantly occurring with a 5.6 earthquake. Afterward, the earthquake rate at the summit dropped, and then slowly began rising again. The summit was flexing up and down!

As the magma withdrew from the reservoir beneath Kilauea summit, it drained into the LERZ and pulled away the support of the rock above it, so that the rock began to collapse. One theory was that the caldera acted as a piston dropping on top of a depressurized magmatic system. In other words, the caldera floor could no longer support its own weight. After an explosive event, the stress on the faults around Halema'uma'u were reduced, resulting in fewer earthquakes. Then, stress began to increase again—

ultimately, the collapse events averaged about every 28 hours. Remarkably, the events seems to register almost always as 5.2 to 5.4 magnitude events.

The ash plumes, however, began to be smaller. It was theorized that after many collapse events and rockfalls, rock rubble from the crater rim had filled the vent, blocking it so that ash could not escape. That was the good news, but the bad news was that if enough pressure built up, a tremendous explosion blasting all the rubble for miles around could take place. Evidently, this scenario had played out in the distant past.

As magma continued to withdraw, the area of subsidence increased. In other words, the ground much further out beyond the caldera began to be affected. That's why cracks began appearing in the roads in Volcano Village.

The scientists were scratching their heads. There were no historical antecedents to predict with any level of certainty what was going to happen. One major theory was that the that the summit was draining with a background trend of subsidence, and happening concurrently, a cyclic pressurization and release of energy that was flexing the overlying rock. Up and down, up and down. But overall we seemed to be going down in increasingly larger and larger steps.

We were experiencing a snapshot in time. Kilauea rose out of the sea a half-million years ago, and is projected to grow to be as high as Mauna Loa, some day far off in the future. Far off! For if lava continues to cover the island at a depth of 30 feet, how many layers will it take to make to to 10,000 feet?

Alarmingly, emissions from the summit ceased, but quakes continued at the rate of more than 300 per day. The vent at Halema'uma'u was blocked. People began to get nervous. Was an unprecedented in-our-lifetime explosion going to occur?

It has happened before.

The Keanakako'i Ash deposits, which are the ash layers around Kilauea caldera, are now believed to have been deposited by *pyroclastic flows* between about 1500 and 1790.

To our disbelief, the old overlook at Kilauea summit plunged into the caldera. Interestingly, most of the quakes were only felt by those near the summit, those of us here in the Village and in the Golf Course. Even the 5.2's were not felt by people in lower Puna.

Interesting question: were the explosive collapses caused by quakes, or were the quakes causing the explosions? A case of which comes first, the chicken or the egg? We never did find out. At any rate, we up here at the summit began to expect our 5.2 daily.

On June 9, two steam plumes heralded the ocean flow front, with a thermal up-welling extending 1000 yards out to sea. Fissures 9 and 10 were steaming and degassing. Pu'u O'o registered 12 rock falls, producing pinkish orange dust plumes.

So it continued for the next few days—the vigorous lava flow to the sea, covering everything in its path, the rockfalls and quakes at the summit, shaking our bones and cracking our roads, terrifying our animals, the subsidence of Kilauea caldera floor threatening a pyroclastic surge, the laze, the Pele's hair accumulation, the building of a new bay at Kapoho, the destruction of homes and farms. By the afternoon of June 12, the fountaining of Fissure 8 had produced a 115 feet high spatter cone. A good question was how far down had the magma receded from the summit? But no one could answer. No one knew for certain how much magma had been stored there.

If all the magma emptied out, would the eruption cease? Or would magma from the core of the Earth continue to rise up and feed the eruption? So many questions without answers.

By June 15, Halema'uma'u crater had enlarged to a hole 0.8 mile in dimension, with a depth of 1210 feet, three times deeper than before, and a 5.3 explosion occurred in the summit resulting in a plume 10,000 high.

By June 16, 467 homes were destroyed. Thousands of people were displaced. Animals were lost. The land was withered. Inward slumping of the rim and walls of Halema'uma'u crater continued, with another gas and ash explosion.

By the 17th, 533 homes were destroyed, and lava had covered 5,914 acres (9.24 square miles).

By the 20th, lava had added 380 acres of new land in the sea at the Kapoho coastline. At some point, Halema'uma'u parking lot had fallen into the crater.

By June 26, the spatter cone was now 180 feet tall and fountains were rising above 180 feet. Halema'uma'u was now one kilometer across and 85 meters deep. The subsidence at the summit seemed to be affecting the ancient caldera, whose edges are right along Highway 11 near the Park entrance. Cracks began to appear in Volcano Golf Course subdivision, less than a mile from Kilauea caldera.

By the 30th, it began to occur to us that we at the summit were in more danger than we had thought. Volcanologist Don Swanson, at a community meeting, compared the present collapse of the summit to the 1500 CE summit collapse. Had that collapse been in stages, as it appeared to be collapsing now, or was it a sudden collapse?

Ever heard of a pyroclastic flow? Pompeii and Herculaneum were consumed by pyroclastic surges, as well as the entire town of St. Pierre on Martinique in 1902, killing everyone but two people. A pyroclastic flow, or surge, is a fast-moving current of hot gas and volcanic matter that moves away from a volcano at speeds of up to 430 miles per hour with temperatures of 1, 830 F.

You can't outrun a pyroclastic flow! I did the calculations. Here in the Village, we would have 30 seconds to get out! Ha!

Kilauea volcano previously had been thought to be an effusive volcano primarily. An effusive eruption is a type of volcanic eruption in which lava steadily flows out of a volcano onto the ground. Effusive eruptions differ from explosive eruptions, where magma is violently fragmented when expelled from a volcano. *But Don Swanson, after years of study, hinted that maybe Kilauea was actually more often an explosive volcano—just in recorded history, which is only a moment in geologic time, it had been effusive, relative peaceful, giving folks time to get out of Pele's way.*

Because Kilauea's surface is covered by young deposits, only the past 2500 years is well known. Effusive flows were the norm until 2200 years ago, when the Powers caldera, the precursor to the present Kilauea caldera, which was closer to the Golf Course, formed. That caldera collapsed to at least 620 meters (2010 feet) deep, where magma interacted with external water to trigger powerful phreatomagmatic (water and magma) eruptions. Explosive eruptions lasted almost 1200 years, producing the tephra around Uēkahuna, the site of the Observatory. Between 850 and 950 CE, the most powerful explosion known occurred, sending rocks weighing 4.4 kg (9.7 lbs) flying at least 3 miles from the summit, and some golf ball-sized rocks hit the coast, 18 km (11 miles) away!

It was a new way of thinking about the volcano. We realized we had been complacent, not really understanding Kilauea's history. *Kilauea had two faces, and we had just seen one of them.*

On July 5th, Highway 11 at the 30-mile marker near Volcano Country Club was closed due to volcano damage. The road was repaired but the following day, more damage occurred and had to be repaired. We're talking BIG cracks in the road. Hawai'i Volcanoes Observatory and Civil Defense called a town meeting in Volcano Village to discuss the possible large scale explosion resulting from the caldera collapse and the possibility of a pyroclastic flow!

There was a mixture of anxiety and disbelief. Volcano residents realized that their property values had dropped to zero, and tourism had dropped to near zero, not a fun realization for folks who had been living for years on the tourist bounty of the volcano.

By July 11, a lobe of lava had reached within 2000 feet of Ahalanui Beach park. A lobe was advancing toward Kua O Ka La Charter School.

By July 12, it was clear that the explosive events at the summit were followed by a surge in activity from Fissure 8 a few hours later. The collapse events at the summit began to get further and further apart, between 30 and 45 hours apart now.

By July 17, the floor of Halemaʻumaʻu Crater had dropped 450 m (about 1480 ft) since May 10 when the lava lake surface disappeared from view.

By July 18, an ʻaʻa flow rode over the flow that was entering the sea. It was about 700 m (0.4 mi) from Isaac Hale Park. By the 20th, it was 400 m (0.25 mi) from the boat ramp at Isaac Hale Park.

On the 22nd, State Highways reported that an 8:53 p. m. collapse event caused additional damage to Highway 11 between the 28 and 32 Mile Markers near Volcano. On the 23rd, the flow was 500 meter (0.3 miles) from the boat ramp at Isaac Hale Park.

We were biting our nails! Some were praying. Some were making offerings to Pele. Some were cursing her.

By July 26, lava movement in the channel was sluggish. The flow was less than 175 m (0.1 mi) from the boat ramp at Isaac Hale. By July 30, Fissure 8 lava was still moving in an open channel southeast of Kapaho Crater, where it crusted over and fed riverlets of lava that entered the sea. Isaac Hale boat ramp had still not been taken, but it seemed inevitable.

I had become interested in the ancient caldera. I had never heard of it before. Where were its boundaries? Was it possible that the crater could collapse to the boundaries of the ancient caldera?

I began to seriously consider that we might have to evacuate at some point. Where would I go?

On July 29, the rangers hinted that Jaggar Museum might be beyond recovery, due to earthquake damage. Chain of Craters Road, the only emergency evacuation route from Kalapana, had developed deep cracks, some tens to hundreds of feet deep. On August 1, the fire station located within the Park was abandoned and relocated to Volcano Village.

It wasn't looking good. Village residents were warned to be ready to evacuate. I drew up my list of what I could fit into my Mazda Miata, not much after three cats!

What's important to take? Besides my cats, I decided on my documents, my weighted blanket and favorite pillow, my favorite sweaters, a statue of Buddha, and my computer. With careful packing, I could fit that much into my car. The cats weren't going to like it! Everything else would be left to Madam Pele.

Because Highway 11 at the Park was taking a big hit, a new road out of the Golf Course was planned. Bad news for me, it was my favorite bike route! I was pissed! Pele had already taken my hikes in Kilauea Iki, my climbs to the top of Mauna Ulu, my treks through the Enchanted Forest, my solitary ambles through Pele's Playground. Instead of my pastoral bicycle ride in the country passing cows and horses and wild pigs and old barns, I would have to surrender it to giant trucks and the fast speed of cars racing to Hilo or Kona.

Not happy!

On August 2, multiple overflows occurred—one headed toward Noni Farms Road and the other toward Kapoho Cone, both igniting vegetation fires. During overflights, lava in the main channel appeared to be at a lower level. Since May 16, Halema'uma'u Crater's depth had more than tripled and the diameter had doubled. The island that had formed offshore by the lava on July 13 was increased to a peninsula, and attached to the coast.

Anxiety was in the air. Tourism had been reduced to nothing, and our island relies on tourists dollars. Farms had been destroyed—almost the entire papaya crop of the Island had been wiped out. The land in the LERZ was parched and toxic gasses were affecting all inhabitants. Thousands were in evacuation centers. Animals were missing and abandoned.

It seemed a nightmare.

August 4!

A big change! But what did it mean? On that wonderful day, the lava was greatly reduced. Also, changes in the summit occurred—the rate of earthquakes at the summit decreased greatly and no collapse occurred. Also, deformation was greatly decreased. The lava was still flowing but there were no overflows. Lower lava levels continued through the next day and helicopter overflights confirmed significant reduction in lava output from Fissure 8.

The summit was quiet!

Was it over?

Did we dare to think it?

The interval between collapse explosions had gotten longer and longer. Was the volcano building up for something bigger? Or was is slowing?

We dared to hope! Yet we also feared.

It held!

On August 6, overflights reported a weak to moderate bubbling lava lake could be seen within the Fissure 8 cone, plus a weak gas plume, and a completely crusted lava channel! Lava continued to ooze but slowly through some of the lobes, and the boat ramp at Isaac Hale Park appeared spared. Pele had come within 0.1 mile of it. The summit was still quiet.

We were warned that it could just be a pause. We went from 500-700 earthquakes a day to 100 quakes, the majority which were no longer at the summit, but in Pahala, Mauna Loa, and Pu'u O'o.

Things were quite. Normal. Normal?

Ha, I thought, how long until the Park reopens?

Other people began conjecturing the same. The last info we had received from the Park was that it would be at least one month after the area was deemed safe before it could reopen. There was a lot of damage; small sections at a time would have to be reopened.

Quiet remained on August 8. We were warned by USGS, "It remains too early to tell whether this is just a pause in activity."

On August 8, we again were warned, *"Summit and LERZ changes considered together imply that the rate of magma leaving the summit to feed the Lower East Rift Zone eruption has decreased. How long this condition will persist is unknown. It is possible that outflow will pick up again, resulting in renewed summit area deflation leading to another collapse event and renewed eruption vigor on the LERZ. HVO will continue to monitor for any signs of change in activity."*

On August 9, conditions were holding. Lava output from Fissure 8 remained low, with a crusted lava pond deep within. Small streams of lava continued to ooze into the ocean. The summit remained quiet except for a few small rockfalls.

On the 10th, the lava pond in Fissure 8 cone had receded to about 40 m (130 feet) below the highest point on the cone's rim. There were less than 5 earthquakes per hour at the summit.

Things were looking better!

I started dreaming of my hikes in Kilauea Iki.

August 11 we were again warned that the eruption might only be paused. Two ponds of lava were observed in Fissure 8 cone—one was crusted over but the other was slowly circulating. There was a gas plume and steaming from the inactive fissures. Quakes at the summit had decreased to only 2-3 per hour. By August 12, the only red lava was an oozing at the ocean, while fresh black sand that had been created when the lava hit the sea and shattered in the surf was being transported toward the south by currents and accumulating in the Pohoiki boat harbor.

On August 13, USGS sent out the following: *"Although the lull in eruptive activity on the LERZ continues, it is common for eruptions to go through periods of diminished output, or to pause completely, only to return with renewed vigor days, weeks, later. Resumption of the activity on the LERZ could occur at any time, and residents should remain informed and heed Hawaii County Civil Defense messages and warnings."*

We held our breath!

Was a catastrophic explosion at the summit in the making, or was it over? Pau?

By August16, Kilauea had been quiet for over a week. Collapse events at the summit had ceased, and Fissure 8 had stopped flowing. On the 19th, the alert level changed from WARNING to WATCH! However, as USGS warned, *"the change does not mean with absolute certainty that the LERZ eruption or summit collapses are over. It remains possible that eruption and collapse activity could resume."*

On August 24, overflights observed a change in the vent at Fissure 8—gas jets were spattering from incandescent areas deep within the cone. *"This activity is an indication that the lower East Rift Zone eruption may be paused rather than pau (over)"* USGS warned. However, sulphur dioxide emissions at both the summit and the lower east rift zone were drastically reduced; it was the lowest since 2007.

By August 28, the number of quakes and ground deformation at the summit were negligible. A small lava

197

pond was visible deep with Fissure 8 cone. No one was sure what that meant.

To top it all off, now we were in the middle of a hurricane!

On the 29th, the morning overflight couldn't detect any incandescence in Fissure 8 cone, nor was there any lava entering the ocean. Also, sulphur dioxide at the summit and in the rift zone had greatly diminished. But by September 1 there was incandescence in the cone and also spattering of lava in the crater floor, now of the size 65 by 15 meters (210 by 45 feet).

For the next two weeks, incandescence in the cone appeared and disappeared, as well as minor lava flows confined within the cone. It seemed a pattern, and, as humans do, we got used to it, and accepted it as the new norm.

About Fissure 8. Fissure 8, the 100 foot cinder cone that appeared as one of 24 cracks and spouted lava 200 feet tall, and wreaked so much havoc and destruction, deserves its own name. Names in Hawaii are important. In fact, there is an entity in charge of selecting names for geographic features in the islands. The Hawaii Board of Geographic Names doesn't propose names, but selects from names submitted by native Hawaiians, especially those who have ties to an area where a geographic name is being proposed. But a first proposal was received—from a Nevada business owner who suggested the name—Puu Leilani. However, after dozens of submitted names and a two year process, Fissure 8 was name: Ahu'aila'au. The name refers to the altar of the volcano deity 'Aila'au.

'Aila'au, largely consigned to the margins of cultural memory, was the volcanic deity that lived in Hawaii before Pele came. Some however, believe that Fissure 8 heralds his return. Some elders and kumu hula even had dreams that Fissure 8 was the work of this older god. Interestingly, volcanologists say that the magma at the start of the eruption was of a more ancient origin.

The aftermath.

Seven hundred homes covered in lava. Jobs lost. Businesses destroyed. Many people moved away, as far as the Mainland. Hopes and dreams dashed. Some were angry and bitter. Others were undefeated, and looked forward to new lives.

On the other hand, the emergency response by our island community was a model of aloha for the world. We the people came together to do for the people. Within a day of the first evacuations, our community was feeding and providing shelter and clothing for our displaced neighbors. Rescuers hiked 8.5 miles out and back across the barely cooled lava to save trapped animals on the flows, and raised money to rent helicopters and boats to go in and get them. Hundreds of people stepped forward to foster and adopt frightened and sickened animals.

What does it mean to live on the world's most active volcano?

We forget. We built one of the most densely populated developments on the very land which has the highest probability of lava inundation. Why?

Complacency. Ignorance. Inexperience. When Leilani Estates and much of lower Puna was developed in large subdivisions in the 1950's, some of which actually straddle the rift zone, there had not been a destructive eruption for years. The old chants warning of the dangers of impetuous and unpredictable Pele had not been heeded, or were regarded as quaintly archaic folklore.

One wonders about the old chants, the oral tradition which describes Goddess Pele as formidable, awesome, to be respected. For the ancient Hawaiians regarded themselves as stewards of the land, as opposed to the Western idea of people owning the land, of having the land, of controlling the land. For the ancients, if Pele were to come, the land was hers to take. They didn't take it personally; it wasn't a personal disaster. They could steward another parcel of land. For Westerners, with land ownership very defined—indeed, a piece of paper owns the land—the loss of land is a personal catastrophe.

What is important now is that Fissure 8, 'Aila'au, is...sleeping?

We can breathe deeply.

As far as everyone is concerned, the eruption is over!

Pau!

Or not?

No!

Because, Kilauea has a long, long history of pauses between eruptive events. Kilauea is still a youngster, between 300,000 and 600,000 years old. Kohala, the oldest volcano on the Big Island, was active for almost 900,000 years before going extinct.

We know the volcano will erupt again.

And again.

Time will tell when.

And now, for something personal.
For those of you who like a little metaphysical.
Hope you enjoy it! Written during the 2018 eruption.

Another Day in Paradise

Woke up this morning and read the news—the President hid in a bunker, riots had grown worse across the country, cities were burning, looting was rampant, vandals were demolishing whole neighborhoods, destroying where the people shop for their food, where they play in their parks, where their children go to school. Transportation has ground to a stop, the police are attacking the protesters, the protesters are attacking the police. Violence. Frenzy. Chaos. Shootings and killings now.

And lurking in the wings, insidiously, assuredly, Covid-19. Covertly waiting for the pickings.

All these things seem no more real than a dream, for I am 3000 miles away from it all, in Hawaii, the closest place on Earth, people say, to paradise.

Paradise. I have always loved the word.

Paradisaical. A place or state ideal or idyllic. Heavenly.

In Islam, in the Qur'an, paradise is 'Al Firdaus, a garden of happiness and peace, a sumptuous gold and bejeweled place where one's every wish is granted, and the highest place in paradise is a mountain from which sacred waters flow. For Christians it is the Garden of Eden, a garden of God, where the Tree of Life grows. For the ancient Egyptians, it is the fields of Aaru, a land of ideal hunting and farming grounds. For the Celts, Mah Meall was an island where there is no sickness or death but eternal youth and beauty and eternal happiness. For the ancient Greeks, it was the Elysian fields, the Isles of the

Blessed; for the Aztecs it was Tamoanchan, birthplace of the goddess of beauty, Xochiquetzal.

With a thankful heart that I am here in this island paradise, I bike to the National Park, which has been closed for months, due to the virus, but has just partially reopened. One trail that has reopened happens to be one I routinely hiked before the shutdown. I missed it! I will leave my bike hitched to a tree and will hike through the Hawaii rainforest as far as four miles down slope toward the sea and back up again. In all the years I have been hiking it, I have run across few other people; mostly I have it to myself.

The Hawaiian rainforest is one of the most benign places on Earth. The ancients walked it barefoot, and one still can. Before Western contact, and invasive species, there were no plants with thorns—there were no predators for which a plant needed to protect itself, and so plants did not evolve thorns or spikes. Before that, before humans came here, there were flightless birds as tall as a small man; they didn't need wings—they had no predators. There were no snakes. There were no mosquitoes. There were no rats.

The rainforest is a place of moment-by-moment change—of course, all things change moment-by-moment but in the rainforest. change is magical and occurs right before one's eyes. The constant flitting of birds from tree to tree, warbling and cawing and peeping and twittering, the fluttering of leaves, the light peeking through the trees throwing dazzling golden spheres that pierce the dark forest, or opening up into magical illuminated circles revealing fairy rings made of puffballs and stinkhorns and toadstools and nurse logs nurturing baby ferns and mosses and saplings, the wind rustling or whistling or whispering through the giant tree ferns as tall as 30 feet, their branches creaking and falling through the foliage—all this bedazzles the senses.

The rainforest can be as enchanted as a fairy land—one can sit on a cozy tuft of grass savoring the eye candy sylvan textures—nubby, downy, chalky, filigreed, frilly, crusty, feathery, furry—and the earthy colors—golds and coppers and rusty browns and every shade of green, with splashes here and there of turquoise and red or orange algae—half expecting elves to pop out at any moment, or one might stretch out on a moss covered fallen log softer than a baby's blanket and soak up some rays while mesmerized by the light dappling the leaves of the 'Olapas, whose bright green leaves flutter in the merest of breezes, evoking the graceful movement of the hula dancers.

Just as often, or more often, because it is not called the rainforest for nothing, it is raining. I love hiking through the jungle in the rain. On a rainy, windy day in the jungle, I am sure to have it all to myself. A jungle storm thrills me, and I have been hiking with lightning bolts crashing down all around me, expecting any moment the next bolt to portend my last breath. Today is a brilliant sunny day, but it has rained the night before, and the jungle glistens with silvery sparkling dewdrops, as if the forest goddess Laka, who is also the goddess of hula, danced through the dawn sprinkling diamonds from her holy hands.

Hawaiians have more than 200 words for *ua*, rain—from the fine, light rain called *kili noe*, or the even finer gradation of rain, rain so light you cannot feel it on your skin, called *kili 'ohu*, to the *ua lanipili*, the torrential downpour. The fragrance of the rain, the fierceness or gentleness, the sound, the rhythm, the feel, the duration—all of these combine to give each rain an identity. There is the light moving rain, the fine windblown rain, the chilly rain, the spraying rain, the thunderless rain, the large-dropped rain, the slanting rain, the surprise rain, the rain of rainbows. Rains are often specific to places, and are immortalized in song and dance.

Rain is considered a blessing in Hawaii—a rain on a parade, on a party or wedding, is considered to be a good omen, a blessing, and no Hawaiian decries the rain ever. Water itself, *wai*, has always been valued as precious by a people who did not always live near a fresh water source, and had only calabashes, gourds, in which to store rain water. Even the word for wealth in Hawaiian is *waiwai*, abundance of water. All the rainforests of our planet are indeed precious jewels. They produce our oxygen and clean our atmosphere; the climate and the global water cycle are intimately interlinked. Ranching, agriculture, poaching, damming, logging, mining and other human activities are destroying the planet's rainforests at a nefarious rate. Can humans survive without the rainforests?

Another terrible threat is invasive species. Now Hawaii is home to half of the planet's top invasive species, including both plants and animals. In a land of perfect abundance and perfect conditions for life, any living thing that makes its way here thrives and proliferates.

That includes viruses.

Island people know too well what can happen with an epidemic. I also am all too aware of what can and will happen if Covid-19 gets its sinister foot in the door. The cultural memory of waves of disease—venereal disease, cholera, influenza, mumps, measles, whooping cough, small pox and leprosy, which all but obliterated the Hawaiian people—have urgently united the public response to virtually isolating Hawaii from the rest of the world, even at the expense of destroying the economy, which is tourist-based. The Hawaii infection rate is currently among the lowest in the U.S. thanks to tough quarantine policies, but the unemployment rate has increased 1,100 per cent from a year ago, so that the people of the islands are hurting.

All these global problems, probably insolvable, weigh on my mind as I bike to the Park.

But once I open the gate, and enter into the lush verdant jungle, all problems disappear! Today is what is real! Today I am back in the magic of the rainforest! I feel like I am meeting up with and old and dear friend! Of course, it's only been three months since the Park closed, but it seems like it has been much longer.

I wonder that I am so lucky!

For a moment I feel guilty. I wonder, why do I get to enjoy this day of abundance? Why am I here, in this paradise today, and not somewhere else, in a different reality? Maybe a place where there is no water, no rain, where the land is parched and dry and hot and barren.

Do I choose this reality? Or does it choose me?

One's life, Buddha said, is a reflection of one's mind. All this, he would say, all this forest that you so love, the birds in the trees, the toadstools, the staghorns, the lacy ferns and velvety mosses and Lilliputian liverworts and hornworts, the infinite textures and rainbow of earth colors is only a projection of your own mind. It is not outside of you. You are not in the forest. The forest is in you.

I've heard this many times by now, this teaching by the Tathagatha. All things have the nature of mind, he said. You, your mind, creates everything.

Is it really true?

As I enter through the gate, into the jungle, I decide I will make an experiment. After all, that's what Buddha said to do, to test if what he said is true. Buddhism, unlike other world religions, is experiential. Not a religion at all, it is a pathway in the mind.

I decide to try, to really try, to see that this incredible display of light and form is really a projection of my own mind.

I am not in the forest.
The forest is in me.

I chant these words as a mantra and focus my mind and my senses on the present like I have never done before. I march along, swinging my arms to the rhythm of my long legs, imagining that it is so—that this forest—the birds, the birdsong, the chirp of the crickets, the light—*it's all in me*. This path I am treading, strewn with golden and coppery fallen leaves and a light dusting of red from lehua blossoms, seems as if it were laid out just for me. I think, *this path is in me. It is not outside of me.*

The sages have said that nature reveals the dharma, the Truth. The birds, the trees, the flowers, the sun, the moon, the stars—they are all chanting the Truth. The Buddha himself told his disciples to go into the forest and practice Truth at the foot of a tree. He himself, of course, attained enlightenment beneath a tree. Spiritual texts record a number of beings who have become enlightened merely by listening to bird songs, or to the wind in the trees, or by contemplating a flower. Once, a sage understood the true nature of reality when a flock of geese flew over his head, so that he swooned into ecstasy.

I stop and carefully examine a bright red lehua blossom, the red pom-pom that adorns the ubiquitous gnarly 'Ohi'a trees. Every forest plant, indeed everything in nature—the stones, the flowers, the animals, the stars—has a story, in Hawaii. The story of the lehua is that once there was a handsome man named 'Ohi'a, with whom Pele, the fire goddess, fell in love. But he did not return her love, for he was in love with a woman named Lehua. Pele, in a fit of jealousy, turned 'Ohi'a into an ugly, gnarled tree. Heart broken, Lehua petitioned the gods to intervene, and caught between a rock and a hard place, so to speak, between Pele's wrath and their pity for Lehua, they compromised. They turned Lehua into the beautiful flower that adorns the 'Ohi'a tree, so that the two lovers could forever be together. It is told that plucking the lehua blossom from the 'Ohi'a tree will cause rain, which is really the tears of Lehua and 'Ohi'a, anguished at being separated. If one must pluck a lehua blossom, it is said, it should not be plucked on the way into the forest, but on the way home, before it rains.

I look at it closely. The blossom is formed by clusters of tiny whitish-gray flowers—the long red filaments, the male part of the plant, the stamens, are what drop to the ground and create the red strewn carpet of the forest. The petals, the pistils, the female parts of the flower, are tiny and at the base of the flower. The very tip of the pistil is the stigma which is the part that will be pollinated by birds: the Japanese White Eye, the I'iwi, the Apapane. I touch the silky red filaments every so slightly, and a showering spray of red fibers falls on the path.

Is this all real? Does it truly exist? I turn and look at all the beauty around me. I listen to the songs of the birds, the wind. Is it real?

It appears to be real.

But Buddha said, "Look. Look more carefully. If you look for the lehua blossom, where is it? You would say it is the flower that you were holding between your fingers. But when the red stamens fell to the ground, where then is the lehua blossom? Is it the petals? And if you pluck off the petals, where is the lehua blossom now? Is it the stem?"

Everything, he said, is made of parts within parts, and when you take away the parts, nothing is left.

A flash of scarlet red alights in the branches above me; an Apapane whistles for her mate, and in the near distance he answers, "I am here. Over here." Buddha would say, "Look at the bird. Now close your eyes, and reopen them. It is not the same bird. The bird you saw a moment ago is already gone, though it appears to be still there—but if you look carefully you will see it is not the same bird. For every moment the bird is changing. There is no real bird there. You can never really catch the bird—any bird you catch will always be a different bird. You too are like the bird. Your own body is not the same body

207

that entered through the gate. Nor is it the same body of just a moment ago."

Even, Buddha would say, if you look carefully, you cannot find your own mind. Your thoughts are no more real than the song of a bird, or the brush of the wind on your arms.

When you look carefully, he would say, there is nothing there. It's just an illusion. Things exist, but not the way they appear to exist. They exist only because you give a name to the appearance of a moment.

The Apapane above me begins to sing, and I know she is singing now for me. "This is your moment," she is singing, "realize it. Realize the Truth. Let me sing it for you."

She lets loose in a melodic trill that goes deep into my heart. And for a moment, I realize it. None of this is real in the way I thought it was. Everything is merely arising and disappearing in my own mind, which itself is like the moon reflected in water, a rainbow bubble, a shadow, a fairy castle.

For a moment the spell is broken!

I see the Truth for what it is!

I am the magician! I am the conjurer! All that I thought was outside of me is on the inside!

An indescribable blissful tingle rushes up my spine.

But just for a moment.

With a rush of wingbeats the lady bird above me takes off.

The spell is not broken! It is cast again!

But now I know. This forest is indeed enchanted! The Apapane, her song, the gold and red strewn path, the diamond dewdrops, the lehua blossoms—all this is my own creation. I have bewitched myself!

Once again, I am ordinary—on the inside, looking out. Looking out at something I take to be real, but I know it is not.

Then something comes to mind, that creator of fairy castles, in the way that thoughts seems to appear at random. (Although of course they are not random at all, but depend upon cause and effect.) I think of the story of the crucifixion, where Jesus hung between two thieves. One of the thieves mocked him, telling him to save himself and them, if he were the Messiah. But the other thief said, "Jesus, remember me when you come into your kingdom." Jesus replied, "Truly I tell you today shalt thou be with me in Paradise."

I think about that word paradise again, and I think about the two thieves on a cross—one chose the darkness, the ordinary world we call real—the realness of rustic nails and quivering flesh and the memory of his misdeeds and a misspent life and the realness of the mocking soldiers at the dusty foot of the cross and the realness of the ominous storm cloud gathering—and the other chose the light—the mystical, magical dwelling place of Christ, the garden of God, Paradise.

I wonder if that's the meaning of the crucifixion, or one of the meanings? That if we open to the magic, we have a choice, and our experience of life depends upon our choice?

With somewhat of a shock I find myself at the gate of the Park again. I have walked eight miles! In what seems only an eye-blink!

Or have I?

I look at the time—yes, it is three hours since I entered the Park.

Amazed at how I could cover eight miles without even knowing it, another thought comes to me.

It is the story of Buddha, the Awakened One, how one day after his daily walk, upon putting his bowl away for the day and sitting down, one of his followers, Subhuti, knelt before him and asked him about the true nature of reality. Buddha's explanation became known as the Diamond Sutra, one of Buddha's best known teachings.

The closing words of what Buddha spoke to Subhuti come to mind:

"So you should view this fleeting world—
A star at dawn, a dewdrop, a bubble in a stream,
A flash of lightening in a summer cloud,
A flickering lamp, a phantom, and a dream."

As I close the gate behind me, I turn and take one last look into the forest until tomorrow. A fine, light mist kisses my arms and my hair, a *kili noe* rain.

*

At the top of Kilauea
Lives the fire of the goddess

Goddess Pele moves
Creaking and crackling as she dances

Pele dances all the way to Puna
The end is in the sea

(from a mele (song) to Pele)

Appendix

Park Visitor Center telephone: 808-985-6000

Park Emergency: 808-985-6170

Hawai'i Volcanoes National Park Map
https://www.nps.gov/havo/planyourvisit/images/e
ntire_park_final.jpg

Current Park Closures
https://www.nps.gov/havo/planyourvisit/conditions.ht
m

**Hawai'i Volcanoes National Park Summit Area
Map**
https://www.nps.gov/havo/planyourvisit/images/H
AVO-8-7-15-summit.jpg

Hawai'i Volcanoes National Park Kahuku Unit
https://www.nps.gov/havo/planyourvisit/images/2012_Kah
uku_map.jpg

National Parks on the Island of Hawai'i
https://www.nps.gov/havo/planyourvisit/images/m
ap_islandcolored_2005_300dpi_lg.jpg

Kahuku Unit Information

https://www.nps.gov/havo/planyourvisit/kahuku-hikes.htm

Island Map

https://www.google.com/maps/place/Hawai'i+Volcan oes+National+Park+Kahuku+Unit/@19.420186,-155.7128057,10z/data=!4m13!1m7!3m6!1s0x7953d6adb4 207fc3:0xbdefd717795aec2!2sHawaii+Volcanoes+Nation al+Park,+HI+96778!3b1!8m2!3d19.3833355!4d-155.2000045!3m4!1s0x7951

Back Country Hiking

https://www.nps.gov/havo/planyourvisit/hike_bc.htm

Pua Po'o Lava Cave Information

http://www.fhvnp.org/institute/wild-caves-exploration/

808-985-7373

Special Permit Form (weddings, ash scattering, etc.)

https://www.nps.gov/havo/learn/management/upload/Sup_ Application_508.pdf

Kilauea Military Camp

Tele--808-967-8333.
http://kilaueamilitarycamp.com/

Volcano Art Center

Gallery 808-967-7566

Niaulani Campus 808-967-8222

http://www.volcanoartcenter.org./

Cooper Community Center

http://www.thecoopercenter.org/#!

Volcano House

808-756-9625

Hawaiivolcanohouse.com

Namakanipaio Campground

866-536-7972 (Volcano House administered)

General information on the Park and environs

http://www.VolcanoVillageHawaii.com/

Mahalo!

Mahalo nui, thank you very much, for reading my guide. I wish I could take everyone of you on a hike through this magical land! I truly hope you have a most wonderful time visiting Kilauea, this very special place on our planet, and I hope you get to come again. Maybe I'll see you on the trail!

Ho 'ola 'i manu i ke aheahe.
"The birds poise quietly in the gentle breezes."

Pause to enjoy the beauty all around you.
Be at peace with the world.

Aloha!

***

Other works by Uldra Johnson

Bones of Love, Stories of Old Hawaii

The Insider's Guide to the Best Beaches of the Big Island

The Cry Room

Ghosts in the Palm of My Hand

How the Universe Made Love to Petal Andersohn

The Wishfulfillling Jewel

Spiritual Not Religious

Hula Angel (A Dream Comes True) (La'akea Johnson)

Made in the USA
Coppell, TX
05 November 2022

85823843R00125